ALARM and HOPE

ALARM and HOPE

Andrei D. Sakharov

Edited by Efrem Yankelevich
and Alfred Friendly, Jr.

VINTAGE BOOKS

A DIVISION OF RANDOM HOUSE

NEW YORK

First Vintage Books Edition, December 1978

Copyright © 1978 by Alfred A. Knopf, Inc.
All rights reserved under International and Pan-American
Copyright Conventions. Published in the United States by
Random House, Inc., New York, and simultaneously in
Canada by Random House of Canada, Limited, Toronto.
Originally published in the U.S.A. as Trevoga i Nadezhda by
Khronika Press, New York. Copyright © 1978 by Khronika
Press. First English Language Edition published simultaneously in
hardcover by Alfred A. Knopf, Inc., December 1978.

Library of Congress Cataloging in Publication Data
Sakharov, Andreï Dmitrievich, 1921–
    Alarm and hope.

    Translation of Trevoga i nadezhda.
    Includes index.
    1. International relations—Addresses, essays, lectures.
2. Civil/rights—Russia—Addresses, essays, lectures. 3. Civil
rights (International law)—Addresses, essays, lectures. I. Title.
JX1395.S26533   1978   323.4'0947   78-64493
ISBN 0-394-72734-7

Grateful acknowledgment is made to the following for
permission to use previously printed material:
"Peace, Progress, and Human Rights," © 1975 by the
Nobel Foundation
"Alarm and Hope," © H. Aschehoug & Co. (W. Nygaard)
A/S, 1978.

Cover design by Paul Gamarello

Manufactured in the United States of America

Contents

Foreword to the
Russian Language Edition

The collection of documents that follows was compiled by Efrem Yankelevich, my son-in-law, friend, close associate, and active participant in the struggle for human rights in the USSR. The collection covers a period of slightly over one year, extending up to August 1, 1977.[*] It contains all my public statements during that time, appeals to Soviet and foreign public figures and organizations, interviews preserved in either written or taped form, and an article written by me for a collection of essays by Nobel Peace Prize winners. Owing to the peculiar conditions of our life and work, the editing and annotation of this book was not a trivial matter. Yankelevich's exceptional conscientiousness, his personal experience, and his detailed knowledge of many of the people and events in this narrative were invaluable for the task.

This book covers a critical period in the international struggle for human rights. I believe that the materials published here, taken as a whole, are of a definite and timely social interest which transcends purely scholarly concerns.

Andrei D. Sakharov
August 29, 1977

[*] The present edition includes materials dating from both before and after this period, through December 1977, as well as an Afterword by Prof. Sakharov written in May 1978.—Ed.

Editors' Note

Although based on the original Russian edition, published in 1978 by Khronika Press of New York, this English translation of *Alarm and Hope* presents Andrei Sakharov's 1976–78 public statements in a revised form with certain deletions and two major additions—the text of the 1975 Nobel Prize speech and an Afterword, written especially for this volume. To avoid repetition, duplicative answers to journalists' questions have been dropped from the text, and the interviews themselves have been edited to juxtapose the author's observations to the press with his other, related public statements and initiatives.

The commentary, which appeared as separate notes in the original edition, has also been edited to supply the necessary background to the statements in a more accessible narrative form. It consists largely of basic factual and biographical information about the people and events to which the author refers, but is more extensive in those instances where a specific case serves to illustrate or typify a general problem in the campaign for human rights in the USSR. In addition, a biographical appendix appears after the text; a dagger following a name indicates that the person in question is listed in this appendix.

The editors wish to acknowledge their debt to Catherine Cosman, Lynne Davidson, Esther Kurz, Susan Pederson, and Helen Sen for translation services. We are also grateful to the *Bulletin of the Atomic Scientists,* the Nobel Foundation, the Norwegian Nobel Committee, the *New York Review of Books,* and *The New York Times* for permission to use material copyrighted or originally published by them.

Introduction

A decade ago a pillar of the Soviet Establishment, Andrei Dmitrivich Sakharov, defected from private grace to public heresy. With the publication in the West of his lengthy essay "Thoughts on Progress, Peaceful Coexistence, and Intellectual Freedom," a nuclear physicist who had played a key role in developing the world's first hydrogen bomb turned from the precise challenges of the scientific world to the moral dilemmas of politics and society.

Retribution was swift. His essay circulated from hand to hand in *samizdat* (self-published) manuscript versions in the USSR in May and June 1968. In July it began to appear—in excerpts, at first—in the West. And in August, as Soviet forces were preparing to crush Czechoslovakia's experiment in liberalizing state socialism, Andrei Sakharov was stripped of his security clearance, prohibited from further work on secret projects, and, within a year, transferred back to the Lebedev Institute of Physics, where he had started as a graduate student.

His apostasy and the ostracism it brought on him have made him a symbol, both inside and outside the Soviet Union, of free thought and its price in a closed society. He has not, however, been a passive bystander in this process. Rather, Sakharov the theoretician has transformed himself into Sakharov the activist, a champion of the principles of human rights and of the people who have suffered, even more than he, for those principles.

Sakharov has spoken of his essay as "one of the first statements of its kind from the mute inner recesses of the socialist countries." What made it original, in fact, was not its thoughtful analysis of the factors which divided the two superpowers and those which impelled them toward a historic convergence of peaceful purpose, but its author's status in the hermetic world of Soviet science. When he wrote the essay and circulated it among other free thinkers for comment and criticism, Sakharov was, he recalled five years later, "very far from the basic problems of all of the people and of the whole country . . . in an extraordinary position of material privilege and isolated from the people."

The privileges and isolation were the rewards and the price of his brilliance as a physicist. His exceptional talent had been recognized in 1941 when (at the age of twenty) he was exempted from military duty to finish his university studies, exploited when he was put to work in 1948 with Igor Tamm and others to develop a thermonuclear weapon, and rewarded in 1953 when he was elected, at thirty-two, the youngest full member of the USSR Academy of Sciences. The son of a physics teacher and grandson of another intellectual, Sakharov had known comfort from childhood, when his family saw to it that he had a governess who could teach him German. The comforts he enjoyed at the height of his scientific career included a large salary, a chauffeured car, access to special shopping and housing privileges, and a full-time bodyguard. He was a national asset, recipient (but secretly) of the Stalin and Lenin Prizes and of three separate Orders of Socialist Labor, the highest Soviet civilian award. But he was also obliged to enjoy most of these honors in the seclusion of the nuclear research center in Turkmenia where his highly classified work was done. And his genius in science, it turned out, conferred on him no special influence in political matters.

"Beginning in 1957," he has written, "I felt myself responsible for the problem of radioactive contamination from nuclear explosions." This sense of responsibility found expression first in memoranda used by others in vain attempts to stop Soviet testing. In 1961, after a three-year moratorium, he personally lobbied Nikita Khrushchev, then Premier, against resuming the explosions, only to be told in public to stick to his research and not to meddle in policy matters. The next year, when a powerful test was planned, Sakharov realized that it was both "useless from the technical point of view" and "criminal" in the fallout hazard it risked. "I made desperate efforts to stop it," he has recalled, even threatening to resign and finally calling Khrushchev directly on the eve of the explosion. All attempts failed. "The feeling of impotence and fright that seized me on that day has remained in my memory ever since," Sakharov disclosed at the end of 1973, "and it has worked much change in me as I moved toward my present attitude."

Still, he kept his civic conscience within acceptable confines for several more years. Active in the campaign inside the scientific and political establishments to free genetics and biology from the witch-doctoring of Stalin's favorite, Trofim Lysenko, Sakharov also surfaced in 1966 as a signer of a collective letter to the party hierarchy warning against any rehabilitation of the late dictator. And in that same year—as the humanistic intelligentsia was bringing forth its band of dissenters—Sakharov telegraphed his protest to the Supreme Soviet against a proposed law (subsequently enacted as Article 190.1) designed to punish any expression of free thought. In 1967 he wrote Leonid Brezhnev to condemn the arrests of Aleksandr Ginzburg and Yuri Galanskov and earned a top official's brusque judgment that "as a politician" Sakharov is "inept."

Although these actions brought him into closer and closer contact with the community of dissenters, Sakharov kept his pleadings and protestations inside the channels of the Soviet system until the summer of 1973. Although he had joined two younger scientists, Valery Chalidze and Andrei Tverdokhlebov, in creating the Human Rights Committee in the fall of 1970, its work and his remained targeted primarily at Soviet officials, while other dissenters took their case to the West more and more frequently in the late 1960s and early 1970s. Not until June 1973 did Sakharov begin a regular practice of turning outside the USSR for help and an audience, first with an appeal to UN Secretary General Kurt Waldheim to intercede on behalf of

Leonid Plyushch and Vladimir Borisov, both forcibly confined to psychiatric hospitals for their nonconformist political views. In July he gave a lengthy interview to Olle Stenholm, a Swedish radio correspondent, and in mid-August he was called in by M. P. Malyarov, a Deputy Procurator General of the USSR, to be warned officially to stop meeting with foreigners, because "you are beginning to be used not only by anti-Soviet forces hostile to our country, but also by foreign intelligence."

The warning was followed by a burst of printed vituperation in the Soviet press and by Sakharov's continued —even increased—efforts to draw foreign attention to the plight of individuals and groups persecuted in the Soviet Union, to the persistent violation of human rights he saw around him. That effort, and its rewards and consequences, is the theme of this collection of his recent statements. Unlike two earlier books printed in the United States and the United Kingdom—*Sakharov Speaks* (1974) and *My Country and the World* (1975)—the present volume documents the personal concerns of Sakharov and his friends as much as it does his ideas and thoughts. It reports, in effect, the passage of Andrei Sakharov from analysis to activism.

That transition has been painful. Under stress, Sakharov has lost friends (to emigration and to imprisonment) and sometimes his composure. The mounting fatigue from the daily strain of receiving petitioners, journalists, even surrogate diplomatic emissaries shows in some of his declarations and behavior. The anguish of the petty, and not so petty, harassment of his family takes its toll, and the recurrent feeling that his appeals for justice go unheard prompts bursts of indignation at the practices of Western journalists who are his chief link to public opinion.

Still, his passion is never petulant; the frustrations remain balanced by an enduring optimism. In 1968, he separated his first major essay into two parts: "Dangers" and "The Basis for Hope." The 1977 essay "Alarm and Hope," which gives this collection its title, echoes that pervasive dualism in Sakharov's world view. It is a feature worth exploring at some length, and not only because the documents collected here give evidence that anxiety for the present can coexist with hope for an improved future.

Dissent in a totalitarian society is constantly challenged with its own apparent futility. As Sakharov himself outlines in his Afterword to this volume, critics can be blunt about both the hopelessness of Soviet dissent and its potential for damaging East-West relations. Most such criticism, however, starts from the assumption that dissenters see themselves as reformers engaged in the active pursuit of social change. Paradoxically (because they have acquired a certain political influence on Soviet and Western conduct in foreign affairs), the majority of "those who think differently" in the Soviet Union did not set out to reshape their own society. Nor do they and Sakharov, their best-known spokesman, act in the real expectation of influencing policy and events. Instead, their inner compulsion is a moral one, an obligation to speak out against perceived injustice. It makes them optimists without concrete hope.

Sakharov formulated the motivation clearly in his 1973 interview with Stenholm: "Well, there is a need to create ideals even when you can't see any path by which to achieve them, because if there are no ideals then there can be no hope, and then one would be completely in the dark, in a hopeless blind alley.

"Moreover, we can't know whether there is some kind of possibility of cooperation between our country and the outside world. If no signals about our unhappy situation are sent out, then there cannot be . . . then even the possibility, which might exist, could not be utilized, because we wouldn't know what it was that needed to be changed or how to change it.

"Then there is the other consideration—that the history of our country should serve as some kind of warning. It should hold back the West and the developing countries from committing mistakes on the scale we have done during our historical development. Therefore, if a man does not keep silent it does not mean that he hopes necessarily to achieve something. These are not the same questions. He may hope for nothing but nonetheless speak because he cannot, simply cannot remain silent.

"In almost every specific case of repression we really have no hope, and almost always there is a tragic absence of positive results."

Considering his background as a theoretical rather than experimental scientist, Sakharov's relative indifference to pragmatic considerations is not surprising. (The indifference, however, is only relative; he is careful to document his reports of injustice and cautious to a degree in his rare suggestions of policies the West should adopt in the face of those injustices.) Moreover, given the setting of Soviet society with its obsessive intolerance of even slight political deviations, a nonconformist such as Sakharov can hope at best for moral influence, an historical role, and would be not "inept" but mad to see himself as a politician.

The irony of his persisting in optimism when "we really have no hope" is that his conduct and that of his sympathizers *have* made an impact on their world. The challenge of decency in international affairs which Sakharov posed was given both a personal and a political response by President Jimmy Carter within a month of his taking office. Their exchange provides the focus for this volume. The work of the Helsinki Watchers in the Soviet Union, ardently supported by Sakharov and directly bolstered by his wife, Elena Bonner, drew the West into a far more energetic advocacy of the Final Act's* human-rights provisions than Western statesmen had initially envisioned. Even the release of such political prisoners as Leonid Plyushch, Mikhail Shtern, and Vladimir Bukovsky or the emergency operation on Sergei Kovalev in a prison hospital can be attributed, at least in part, to eventual Soviet sensitivity to the public clamor on their behalf that Sakharov played such a persistent role in developing.

* The Final Act of the Conference on Security and Cooperation in Europe was signed in Helsinki, Finland, on August 1, 1975, by representatives of thirty-three European states, the United States, and Canada. It is variously referred to as the Helsinki Final Act, the Helsinki Accord, and the Helsinki Agreement.

Most of this volume documents that role in one appeal after another for men and women who have been denied justice and free expression. Inevitably, there are few success stories to be found here. Inevitably, there is much repetition. The clash of human dignity and impersonal power is too old a story to promise much novelty. But the record of Sakharov's constant, Sisyphean effort has to be more than a cautionary tale about the persistence of evil. It is also a proof of the wisdom of a much earlier statesman, King William the Silent of the Netherlands, whose motto was: "It is not necessary to hope in order to undertake, nor to succeed in order to persevere."

One of Sakharov's great triumphs, of course, was his designation in October 1975 as recipient of the Nobel Prize for Peace. No one who was present in his cramped Moscow apartment the next day is likely to forget either the siege of journalists asking—vainly—for something new and eloquent to mark the occasion or the brief and tentative visit of a young Norwegian diplomat bearing his ambassador's compliments and a vase of red roses. Diplomats were rare visitors in that undistinguished building; they guarded their immunity in Moscow by not expending it on "internal affairs" of the Soviet state. Journalists were constant callers, on the other hand, but their concerns tended to the transitory—the latest indignity of persecution, the freshest news.

Neither envoy nor reporters were really in a position to recognize the moment for its considerable significance: the symbolic victory of an apostle of open public discussion over the surrounding society and structure of secrecy. For if Sakharov's views of the world have changed over the decade he has spent formulating and reformulating them, one concern has remained constant. In the 1968 essay he wrote that "intellectual freedom is essential to human society—freedom to obtain and distribute information, freedom for open-minded and unfearing debate, and freedom from pressure by officialdom and prejudices." In his 1975

Nobel Lecture, he rephrased and expanded the thought: ". . . I am convinced that international trust, mutual understanding, disarmament, and international security are inconceivable without an open society with freedom of information, freedom of conscience, the right to publish, and the right to travel and choose the country in which one wishes to live."

The Nobel Prize citation recognized this insistent thesis in Sakharov's activity, his unchanging advocacy of the belief that an open world is a safer one. To Westerners familiar with the thinking of Woodrow Wilson or the rhetoric of the Atlantic Charter, the idea is part of conventional liberal wisdom in the twentieth century. It is the democratic ideal translated into international affairs, and it is easy to forget that the ideal is neither universal nor unchallenged. But the truth, of course, is that balance-of-power equations or other variants of realpolitik have frequently been more tempting to superpower policymakers than the quest for the human-rights priorities of openness and individual liberty. And Sakharov has been criticized—not just in the Soviet Union—for overburdening U.S.-Soviet détente with futile moralizing and utopian pursuits.

Sakharov, however, views himself as an advocate of détente, not its enemy. In answering a correspondent's question a year after the Nobel ceremony, he observed that "détente, as it is operating now, is basically a polite form of cold war," but to him its courtesies and restraints are more than camouflage. "We must not forget," he told another reporter two months later, "that only détente created the possibility of exerting even minimal influence on both the domestic and foreign policies of the socialist countries. In the name of détente they are required to accommodate their actions to universal humanitarian standards. It would be a great misfortune to return to the past."

The question is still open, whether or not East-West tensions can be relaxed while one side violates human rights at home and the other insists on their observance everywhere. Sakharov's answer throughout this book is that the question is irrelevant. Either détente furthers the interwoven causes of decency and security or it will simply be a brief historical prelude to the final catastrophe. As an optimist without concrete hope, Sakharov offers in these documents all his reasons for continuing the patient, slow, but determined quest for justice.

In the Nobel Lecture which opens this volume, he sums up his aims and his hope:

"We need reform, not revolution. We need a flexible, pluralist, tolerant society, which selectively and experimentally can foster a free, undogmatic use of the experiences of all kinds of social systems. What is détente? What is rapprochement? We are concerned not with words, but with a willingness to create a better and more decent society, a better world order.

". . . other civilizations, including more 'successful' ones, should exist an infinite number of times on the 'preceding' and the 'following' pages of the Book of the Universe. Yet we should not minimize our sacred endeavors in this world, where, like faint glimmers in the dark, we have emerged for a moment from the nothingness of dark unconsciousness into material existence. We must make good the demands of reason and create a life worthy of ourselves and of the goals we only dimly perceive."

Alfred Friendly, Jr.

ALARM and HOPE

I

Peace, Progress, and Human Rights

The Nobel Peace Prize Lecture, 1975

CITATION FOR THE 1975 NOBEL PEACE PRIZE AWARD

The Nobel Committee of the Norwegian Parliament has awarded Nobel's peace prize for 1975 to Andrei Sakharov.

Sakharov's personal and fearless effort in the cause of peace among mankind serves as a mighty inspiration to all true endeavors to promote peace. Uncompromisingly and forcefully, Sakharov has fought not only against the abuse of power and violations of human dignity in all its forms, but he has with equal vigor fought for the ideal of a state founded on the principle of justice for all.

In a convincing fashion Sakharov has emphasized that the individual rights of man can serve as the only sure foundation for a genuine and long-lasting system of international cooperation. In this manner he has succeeded very effectively, and under trying conditions, in reinforcing respect for such values as all true friends of peace are anxious to support.

Andrei Dmitrivich Sakharov has addressed his message of peace and justice to all peoples of the world. For him it is a fundamental principle that world peace can have no lasting value, unless it is founded on respect for the individual human being in society. This respect has found expression in several international declarations; for example, the UN declaration on the rights of man. Sakharov has demanded that the national authorities of each country must live up to the commitments they have undertaken in signing these declarations.

In the various agreements signed this year by 35 states at the security conference in Helsinki, it was again emphasized that this respect for human dignity was an obligation undertaken by the states themselves. In the agreement the parties acknowledge that respect for human rights and fundamental freedoms is an important factor in the cause of peace, justice, and well-being which is essential to ensure the development of friendly relations and cooperation not only among themselves but among all the countries of the world.

In more forceful terms than others, Andrei Sakharov has warned us against not taking this seriously, and he has placed himself in the vanguard of the efforts to make the ideals expressed in this paragraph of the Helsinki agreement a living reality.

Andrei Sakharov is a firm believer in the brotherhood of man, in genuine coexistence, as the only way to save mankind. It was precisely by means of encouraging fraternization between all peoples, based on truth and sincerity, that Alfred Nobel envisaged the possibilities of creating a safer future for all mankind. When states violate the fundamental precepts of human rights, they are also, in Sakharov's view, undermining the work to promote confidence across national borders.

Sakharov has warned against the dangers connected with a bogus detente based on wishful thinking and illusions. As a nuclear physicist he has, with his special insight and sense of responsibility, been able to speak out against the dangers inherent in the armaments race between the states. His aims are demilitarization, democratization of society in all countries and a more rapid pace of social progress.

Sakharov's love of truth and strong belief in the inviolability of the human being, his fight against violence and brutality, his courageous defense of the freedom of the spirit, his unselfishness and strong humanitarian convictions have turned him into the spokesman for the conscience of mankind, which the world so sorely needs today.

Peace, progress, human rights—these three goals are indissolubly linked: it is impossible to achieve one of them if the others are ignored. This idea provides the main theme of my lecture.

I am deeply grateful that this great and significant award, the Nobel Peace Prize, has been given to me, and that I have the opportunity of addressing you here today. I was particularly gratified at the Committee's citation, which stresses the defense of human rights as the only sure basis for genuine and lasting international cooperation. This idea is very important to me; I am convinced that international trust, mutual understanding, disarmament, and international security are inconceivable without an open society with freedom of information, freedom of conscience, the right to publish, and the right to travel and choose the country in which one wishes to live. I am also convinced that freedom of conscience, together with other civic rights, provides both the basis for scientific progress and a guarantee against its misuse to harm mankind, as well as the basis for economic and social progress, which in turn is a political guarantee making the effective defense of social rights possible. At the same time I should like to defend the thesis of the original and decisive significance of civic and political rights in shaping the destiny of mankind. This view differs essentially from the usual Marxist theory, as well as from technocratic opinions, according to which only material factors and social and economic conditions are of decisive importance. (But in saying this, of course, I have no intention of denying the importance of people's material welfare.)

I should like to express all these theses in my lecture, and in particular to dwell on a number of specific problems affecting the violation of human rights. A solution of these problems is imperative, and the time at our disposal is short.

This is the reason why I have called my lecture "Peace, Progress, and Human Rights." There is, naturally, a conscious parallel with the title of my 1968 article "Thoughts on Progress, Peaceful Coexistence, and Intellectual Freedom,"° with which my lecture, both in its contents and its implications, has very close affinities.

There is a great deal to suggest that mankind, at the threshold of the second half of the twentieth century, entered a particularly decisive and critical historical era.

Nuclear missiles exist capable in principle of annihilating the whole of mankind; this is the greatest danger threatening our age. Thanks to economic, industrial, and

° Included in *Sakharov Speaks* (1974).

scientific advances, so-called "conventional" arms have likewise grown incomparably more dangerous, not to mention chemical and bacteriological instruments of war.

There is no doubt that industrial and technological progress is the most important factor in overcoming poverty, famine, and disease. But this progress leads at the same time to ominous changes in the environment in which we live and to the exhaustion of our natural resources. Thus, mankind faces grave ecological dangers.

Rapid changes in traditional forms of life have resulted in an unchecked demographic explosion which is particularly noticeable in the developing countries of the Third World. The growth in population has already created exceptionally complicated economic, social, and psychological problems and will in the future inevitably pose still more serious problems. In many countries, particularly in Asia, Africa, and Latin America, the lack of food will be an overriding factor in the lives of many hundreds of millions of people, who from the moment of birth are condemned to a wretched existence on the starvation level. Moreover, future prospects are menacing, and in the opinion of many specialists, tragic, despite the undoubted success of the "green revolution."

But even in the developed countries, people face serious problems. These include the pressure resulting from excessive urbanization, all the changes that disrupt the community's social and psychological stability, the incessant pursuit of fashion and trends, overproduction, the frantic, furious tempo of life, the increase in nervous and mental disorders, the growing number of people deprived of contact with nature and of normal human lives, the dissolution of the family and the loss of simple human pleasures, the decay of the community's moral and ethical principles, and the loss of faith in the purpose of life. Against this background there is a whole host of ugly phenomena: an increase in crime, in alcoholism, in drug addiction, in terrorism, and so forth. The imminent exhaustion of the world's resources, the threat of overpopulation, the constant and deep-rooted international, political, and social problems are making a more and more forceful impact on the developed countries too, and will deprive—or at any rate threaten to deprive—a great many people who are accustomed to abundance, affluence, and creature comforts.

However, in the pattern of problems facing the world today a more decisive and important role is played by the global political polarization of mankind, which is divided into the so-called First World (conventionally called the Western world), the Second (socialist), and the Third (the developing countries). Two powerful socialist states, in fact, have become mutually hostile totalitarian empires, in which a single party and the state exercise immoderate power in all spheres of life. They possess an enormous potential for expansion, striving to increase their influence to cover large areas of the globe. One of these states—the Chinese People's Republic—has reached only a relatively modest stage of economic development, whereas the other —the Soviet Union—by exploiting its unique natural resources, and by taxing to the utmost the powers of its inhabitants and their ability to suffer continued privation, has built up a tremendous war potential and a relatively high— though one-sided—economic development. But in the Soviet Union, too, the people's standard of living is low, and civic rights are more restricted than in less socialist countries. Highly complicated global problems also affect the Third World, where relative economic stagnation goes hand in hand with growing international political activity.

Moreover, this polarization further reinforces the serious dangers of nuclear annihilation, famine, pollution of the environment, exhaustion of resources, overpopulation, and dehumanization.

If we consider this complex of urgent problems and contradictions, the first point that must be made is that any attempt to reduce the tempo of scientific and technological progress, to reverse the process of urbanization, to call for isolationism, patriarchal ways of life, and a renaissance based on ancient national traditions, would be unrealistic. Progress is indispensable, and to halt it would lead to the decline and fall of our civilization.

Not long ago we were unfamiliar with artificial fertilizers, mechanized farming, chemical pesticides, and intensive agricultural methods. There are voices calling for a return to more traditional and possibly less dangerous forms of agriculture. But can this be accomplished in a world in which hundreds of millions of people are suffering from hunger? On the contrary, there is no doubt that we need increasingly intensive methods of farming, and we must spread modern methods all over the world, including the developing countries.

We cannot reject the idea of a spreading use of the results of medical research or the extension of research in all its branches, including bacteriology and virology, neurophysiology, human genetics, and gene surgery, no matter what potential dangers lurk in their abuse and the undesirable social consequences of this research. This also applies to research in the creation of artificial intelligence systems, research involving behavior, and the establishment of a unified system of global communication, systems for selecting and storing information, and so forth. It is quite clear that in the hands of irresponsible bureaucratic authorities operating secretly, all this research may prove exceptionally dangerous, but at the same time it may prove extremely important and necessary to mankind, if it is carried out under public supervision and discussion and socio-scientific analysis. We cannot reject wider application of artificial materials, synthetic food, or the modernization of every aspect of life; we cannot obstruct growing automation and industrial expansion, irrespective of the social problems these may involve.

We cannot condemn the construction of bigger nuclear power stations or research into nuclear physics, since energetics is one of the bases of our civilization. In this connection I should like to remind you that twenty-five years ago I and my teacher, the winner of the Nobel Prize for Physics, Igor Yevgenevich Tamm, laid the basis for nuclear research in our country. This research has achieved tremendous scope, extending into the most varied directions, from the classical method for magnetic heat insulation to those for the use of lasers.

We cannot cease interplanetary and intergalactic space research, including the attempts to intercept signals from civilizations outside our own earth. The chance that such experiments will prove successful is probably small, but precisely for this reason the results may well be tremendous.

I have mentioned only a few examples. In actual fact all important aspects of progress are closely interwoven; none of them can be discarded without the risk of destroying the entire structure of our civilization. Progress is indivisible. But intellectual factors play a special role in the mechanism of progress. Underestimating these factors is particularly widespread in the socialist countries, probably due to the populist-ideological dogmas of official philosophy, and may well result in distortion of the path of progress or even its cessation and stagnation.

Progress is possible and innocuous only when it is subject to the control of reason. The important problems involving environmental protection exemplify the role of public opinion, the open society, and freedom of conscience. The partial liberalization in our country after the death of Stalin made it possible to engage in public debate on this problem during the early 1960s. But an effective solution demands increased tightening of social and international control. The military application of scientific results and controlled disarmament are an equally critical area, in which international confidence depends on public opinion and an open society. The example I gave involving the manipulation of mass psychology is already highly topical, even though it may appear farfetched.

Freedom of conscience, the existence of an informed public opinion, a pluralistic system of education, freedom of the press, and access to other sources of information—all these are in very short supply in the socialist countries. This situation is a result of the economic, political, and ideological monism which is characteristic of these nations. At the same time these conditions are a vital necessity, not only to avoid all witting or unwitting abuse of progress, but also to strengthen it.

An effective system of education and a creative sense of heredity from one generation to another are possible only in an atmosphere of intellectual freedom. Conversely, intellectual bondage, the power and conformism of a pitiful

bureaucracy, acts from the very start as a blight on humanistic fields of knowledge, literature, and art and results
eventually in a general intellectual decline, the bureaucratization and formalization of the entire system of education,
the decline of scientific research, the thwarting of all incen-
tive to creative work, stagnation, and dissolution.

In the polarized world the totalitarian states, thanks to
détente, today may indulge in a special form of intellectual
parasitism. And it seems that if the inner changes that we
all consider necessary do not take place, those nations will
soon be forced to adopt an approach of this kind. If this
happens, the danger of an explosion in the world situation
will merely increase. Cooperation between the Western
states, the socialist nations, and the developing countries is
—a vital necessity for peace, and it involves exchanges of
scientific achievements, technology, trade, and mutual economic aid, particularly where food is concerned. But this
cooperation must be based on mutual trust between open
societies, or—to put it another way—with an open mind, on
the basis of genuine equality and not on the basis of the
democratic countries' fear of their totalitarian neighbors.
If that were the case, cooperation would merely involve an
attempt at ingratiating oneself with a formidable neighbor.
But such a policy would merely postpone the evil day, soon
to arrive anyway and, then, ten times worse. This is simply
another version of Munich. Détente can only be assured if
from the very outset it goes hand in hand with continuous
openness on the part of all countries, an aroused sense of
public opinion, free exchange of information, and absolute
respect in all countries for civic and political rights. In
short: in addition to détente in the material sphere, with
disarmament and trade, détente should take place in the
intellectual and ideological sphere. President Giscard
d'Estaing of France expressed himself in an admirable fashion during his visit to Moscow. Indeed, it was worth enduring criticism from shortsighted pragmatists among his
countrymen to support such an important principle.

Before dealing with the problem of disarmament I
should like to take this opportunity to remind you of some of
my proposals of a general nature. First and foremost is the

idea of setting up an international consultative committee for questions related to disarmament, human rights, and the protection of the environment, under the aegis of the United Nations. In my opinion a committee of this kind should have the right to exact replies from all governments to its inquiries and recommendations. The committee could become an important working body in securing international discussion and information on the most important problems affecting the future of mankind. I hope this idea will receive support and be discussed.

I should also emphasize that I consider it particularly important for United Nations armed forces to be used more generally for the purpose of restricting armed conflicts between states and ethnic groups. I have a high regard for the United Nations role, and I consider the institution to be one of mankind's most important hopes for a better future. Recent years have proved difficult and critical for this organization. I have written on this subject in *My Country and the World,* but after it was published, a deplorable event took place: the General Assembly adopted—without any real debate—a resolution declaring Zionism a form of racism and racial discrimination. Zionism is the ideology of a national rebirth of the Jewish people after two thousand years of diaspora, and it is not directed against any other people. The adoption of a resolution of this kind has damaged the prestige of the United Nations. But despite such motions, which are frequently the result of an insufficient sense of responsibility among leaders of some of the UN's younger members, I believe nevertheless that the organization may sooner or later be in a position to play a worthy role in the life of mankind, in accordance with its Charter's aims.

Let me now address one of the central questions of the present age, the problem of disarmament. I have described in detail just what my position is in *My Country and the World.* It is imperative to promote confidence between nations, and carry out measures of control with the aid of international inspection groups. This is only possible if détente is extended to the ideological sphere, and it presupposes greater openness in public life. I have stressed the need for international agreements to limit arms supplies to other states, special agreements to halt production of new weapons systems, treaties banning secret rearmament, the elimination of strategically unbalancing factors, and in particular a ban on multi-warhead nuclear missiles.

What would be the ideal international agreement on disarmament on the technical plane?

I believe that prior to such an agreement we must have an official declaration—though not necessarily public in the initial stages—on the extent of military potential (ranging from the number of nuclear warheads to forecast figures on the number of personnel liable for military service), with, for example, an indication of areas of "potential confrontation." The first step would be to ensure that for every single strategic area and for all sorts of military strength an adjustment would be made to iron out the superiority of one party to the agreement in relation to the other. (Naturally this is the kind of pattern that would be liable to some adjustment.) This would in the first place obviate the possibility of an agreement in one strategic area (Europe, for instance) being utilized to strengthen military positions in another area (e.g., the Soviet-Chinese border). In the second place, potential imbalances arising from the difficulty of equating different weapons systems would be excluded. (It would, for example, be difficult to say how many batteries of the ABM type would correspond to a cruiser, and so on.)

The next step in disarmament would entail proportional and simultaneous de-escalation for all countries and in all strategic areas. Such a formula for "balanced" two-stage disarmament would ensure continuous security for all countries, an interrelated equilibrium between armed forces in areas where there is a potential danger of confrontation, while at the same time providing a radical solution to the economic and social problems that have arisen as a result of militarization. In the course of time a great many experts and politicians have put forward similar views, but hitherto these have not had significant impact. However, now that humanity is faced with a real threat of annihilation in the holocaust of nuclear explosion, I hope that we will not hesitate to take this step. Radical and balanced disarmament is in effect both necessary and possible, constituting an integral part of a manifold and complicated process for the solution of the menacing and urgent problems facing the world. The new phase in international relations which has been called détente, and which appears to have culminated with the Helsinki Conference, does in principle open up certain possibilities for a move in this direction.

The Final Act signed at the Helsinki Conference is particularly noteworthy because for the first time official expression was given to an approach which appears to be the only possible one for a solution of international security problems. This document contains far-reaching declarations on the relationship between international security and preservation of human rights, freedom of information, and freedom of movement. These rights are guaranteed by solemn obligations entered into by the participating nations. Obviously we cannot speak here of a guaranteed result, but we can speak of fresh possibilities that can only be realized as a result of long-term planned activities, in which the participating nations, and especially the democracies, maintain a unified and consistent attitude.

Regarding the problem of human rights, I should like to speak mainly of my own country. During the months since the Helsinki Conference there has been no real improvement in this direction. In fact there have been attempts on the part of hard-liners to "give the screw another turn," in international exchange of information, the freedom to choose the country in which one wishes to live, travel abroad for studies, work, or health reasons, as well as ordinary tourist travel. To illustrate my assertion, I should like to give you a few examples—chosen at random and without any attempt to provide a complete picture.

You all know, even better than I do, that children from Denmark can get on their bicycles and cycle off to the Adriatic. No one would ever suggest that they were "teenage spies." But Soviet children are not allowed to do this! I am sure you are familiar with analogous examples.

The UN General Assembly, influenced by the socialist states, has imposed restrictions on the use of satellites for international TV transmissions. Now that the Helsinki Conference has taken place, there is every reason to deal afresh with this problem. For millions of Soviet citizens this is an important and interesting matter.

In the Soviet Union there is a severe shortage of artificial limbs and similar aids for invalids. But no Soviet invalid, even though he may have received a formal invitation from a foreign organization, is allowed to travel abroad in response to such an invitation.

Soviet newsstands rarely offer non-Communist newspapers, and it is not possible to buy every issue of Communist periodicals. Even informative magazines like *Amerika* are in very short supply. They are on sale only at a small number of newsstands, and are immediately snapped up by eager buyers.

Any person wishing to emigrate from the Soviet Union must have a formal invitation from a close relative. For many this is an insoluble problem—for 300,000 Germans, for example, who wish to go to West Germany. (The emigration quota for Germans is 5,000 a year, which means that one might be forced to wait for sixty years!) The situation for those who wish to be reunited with relatives in Socialist countries is particularly tragic. There is no one to plead their case, and in such circumstances the arbitrary behavior of the authorities knows no bounds.

The freedom to travel and the freedom to choose where one wishes to work and live are still violated in the case of millions of collective-farm workers, and in the situation of hundreds of thousands of Crimean Tatars, who thirty years ago were cruelly and brutally deported from the Crimea and who to this day have been denied the right to return to their homeland.

The Helsinki Accord confirms the principle of freedom of conscience. However, a relentless struggle will have to be carried on if the provisions of this agreement are to be realized in practice. In the Soviet Union today many thousands of people are both judicially and extrajudicially persecuted for their convictions: for their religious faith and their desire to bring up their children in a religious spirit, or for reading and disseminating—often only to a few acquaintances—literature of which the state disapproves, but which from the standpoint of ordinary democratic practice is absolutely legitimate. On the moral plane, there is particular gravity in the persecution of persons who have defended other victims of unjust treatment, who have worked to publish and, in particular, to distribute information regarding both the persecution and trials of persons with deviant opinions and the conditions in places of imprisonment.

It is unbearable to consider that at the very moment we are gathered together in this hall on this festive occasion hundreds and thousands of prisoners of conscience are suffering from undernourishment, as the result of year-long hunger, of an almost total lack of proteins and vitamins in their diet, of a shortage of medicines (there is a ban on the sending of vitamins and medicines to inmates), and of overexertion. They shiver from cold, damp, and exhaustion in ill-lit dungeons, where they are forced to wage a ceaseless struggle for their human dignity and to maintain their convictions against the "indoctrination machine," in fact against the destruction of their souls. The special nature of the concentration-camp system is carefully concealed. The sufferings a handful have undergone, because they exposed the terrible conditions, provide the best proof of the truth of their allegations and accusations. Our concept of human dignity demands an immediate change in this system for all imprisoned persons, no matter how guilty they may be. But what about the sufferings of the innocent? Worst of all is the hell that exists in the special psychiatric clinics in Dnepropetrovsk, Sytchevka, Blagoveshchensk, Kazan, Chernyakhovsk, Orel, Leningrad, Tashkent . . .

There is no time for me today to describe in detail particular trials, or the fates of particular persons. There is a wealth of literature on this subject: may I draw your attention to the publications of Khronika Press in New York, which specializes in reprints of the Soviet *samizdat* periodical *The Chronicle of Current Events* and issues similar bulletins of current information. I should like to mention the names of some of the internees I know. I would ask you to remember that all prisoners of conscience and all political prisoners in my country share with me the honor of the

Nobel Prize. Here are some of the names that are known to me:*

Plyushch, Bukovsky,† Gluzman,† Moroz,† Maria Semyonova,† Nadezhda Svitlichnaya, Stefania Shabatura, Irina Stasiv-Kalinets, Irina Senik, Nijole Sadunaite, Anait Karapetian, Osipov,† Kronid Lyubarsky,† Shumuk,† Vins,† Rumachik, Khaustov,† Superfin,† Paulaitis,† Simutis, Karavanskiy, Valery Marchenko, Shukhevich, Pavlenkov, Chernoglaz, Abankin, Suslenskiy, Meshener, Svitlichny,† Safronov, Rode, Shakirov, Heifetz, Afanasiev, Ma-Khun, Butman, Lukianenko, Ogurtsov,† Sergienko,† Antoniuk, Lupynos, Ruban, Plakhotnyuk, Kovgar, Belov, Igrunov, Soldatov,† Myattik, Kiirend,† Jushkevich, Zdorovy, Tovmasian, Shakhverdian, Zagrobian, Airikian,† Markosian, Arshakian, Mirauskas, Stus, Sverstiuk, Kandyba, Ubozhko, Romanyuk,† Vorobyov, Gel, Pronyuk,† Gladko, Malchevsky, Grazhis, Prishliak, Sapeliak, Kalinets, Suprei, Valdman, Demidov, Bernitchuk, Shovkovy, Gorbachov, Berchov, Turik, Zhukauskas, Bolonkin, Lsovoi, Petrov, Chekalin, Gorodetsky, Chornovil,† Balakhonov, Bondar, Kalinichenko, Kolomin, Plumpa, Jaugelis, Fedoseyev, Osadchy, Budulak-Sharigin, Makarenko,† Malkin, Shtern,† Lazar Lyubarsky, Feldman, Roitburd, Shkolnik, Murzhenko, Fyodorov,† Dymshits, Kuznetsov,† Mendelevich, Altman, Penson, Knokh, Vulf Zalmanson, Izrail Zalmanson, and many, many others. Among those unjustly exiled are Anatoly Marchenko,† Nashpits, and Tsitlyonok.

Mustafa Dzhemilev, Kovalev, and Tverdokhlebov are awaiting trial. There is no time to mention all the prisoners I know of, and there are many more whom I do not know, or of whom I have insufficient knowledge. But their names are all implicit in what I have to say, and I should like those whose names I have not announced to forgive me. Every single name, mentioned as well as unmentioned, represents a hard and heroic destiny, years of suffering, years of struggling for human dignity.

A final solution to persecutions can be based on international agreement—amnesty for political prisoners, for

---

* A dagger indicates that biographical information on the person in question is supplied in the Appendix that follows the text.

prisoners of conscience in prisons, internment camps, and psychiatric clinics as set forth in a UN General Assembly resolution. This proposal involves no intervention in the internal affairs of any country. It would apply to every state on the same basis—to the Soviet Union, to Indonesia, to Chile, to the Republic of South Africa, to Spain, to Brazil, and to every other country. Since the protection of human rights has been proclaimed in the United Nations Declaration of Human Rights, there can be no reason to call this issue a matter of purely internal or domestic concern. In order to achieve this goal, no efforts can be too great, however long the road may seem. And that the road is long was clearly shown during the recent session of the United Nations, in the course of which the United States moved a proposal for political amnesty, only to withdraw it after attempts had been made by a number of countries to expand the scope of the amnesty. I much regret what took place. A problem cannot be removed from circulation. I am profoundly convinced that it would be better to liberate a certain number of people—even though they might be guilty of some offense or other—than to keep thousands of innocent people locked up and exposed to torture.

Without losing sight of an overall solution of this kind, we must fight against injustice and the violation of human rights for every individual person separately. Much of our future depends on this.

In struggling to defend human rights we ought, I am convinced, first and foremost to protect the innocent victims of regimes installed in various countries, without demanding the destruction or total condemnation of these regimes. We need reform, not revolution. We need a flexible, pluralist, tolerant society, which selectively and experimentally can foster a free, undogmatic use of the experiences of all kinds of social systems. What is détente? What is rapprochement? We are concerned not with words, but with a willingness to create a better and more decent society, a better world order.

Thousands of years ago human tribes suffered great privations in the struggle to survive. It was then important not only to be able to handle a club, but also to possess the ability to think intelligently, to take care of the knowledge and experience garnered by the tribe, and to develop the links that would provide cooperation with other tribes. Today the human race is faced with a similar test. In infinite space many civilizations are bound to exist, among them societies that may be wiser and more "successful" than ours. I support the cosmological hypothesis which states that the development of the universe is repeated in its basic characteristics an infinite number of times. Further, other civilizations, including more "successful" ones, should exist an infinite number of times on the "preceding" and the "following" pages of the Book of the Universe. Yet we should not minimize our sacred endeavors in this world, where, like faint glimmers in the dark, we have emerged for a moment from the nothingness of dark unconsciousness into material existence. We must make good the demands of reason and create a life worthy of ourselves and of the goals we only dimly perceive.

The Nobel Lecture was read in Oslo, December 11, 1975, not by Sakharov, but by his wife, Elena Bonner. Sakharov had applied on October 20 for an exit visa to attend the award ceremony and deliver his speech, but his request was refused, according to an official's published statement, "for reasons of security, because A. Sakharov is the possessor of exceptionally important state and military secrets."

Bowing to the inevitable, Sakharov wrote the Nobel Committee of the Norwegian Parliament, designating his wife—who was then in Italy for treatment of advancing glaucoma—to be his official representative. "Over the past years," he wrote, "to a considerable degree her selfless support and help, sometimes her initiative, and our mutual understanding have made possible the public activity for which you have honored me so highly."

Instead of flying to Oslo, Sakharov and a group of friends, including two whom he had wanted invited as his guests to the Nobel ceremonies, went to Vilnius, the postwar capital of Lithuania, for the trial of a close and respected colleague in the human rights movement, the biologist Sergei Kovalev.

II

The Case of Sergei Kovalev

The day the Nobel Peace Prize was formally awarded to him was Sakharov's second day of vigil outside the Lithuanian Supreme Court. Surrounded by his friends from Moscow—except for three women whom police in the capital had put under house arrest after their attempts to take a train to Vilnius—and new acquaintances from Lithuania, such as the Catholic activist Viktoras Petkus,† he stood outside the doors of the courtroom where Sergei Kovalev was on trial for his involvement with The Chronicle of Current Events.

Between the summer of 1972 and the spring of 1974, no new issues of The Chronicle of Current Events, *the dissident information journal which first appeared in April 1968, circulated in samizdat in Moscow. The arrests and convictions of those who had been distributing the human-rights record* (Kronid Lyubarsky†) *and helping to edit it* (Gabriel Superfin†) *had apparently driven their sympathizers into silence and passivity. On May 7, 1974, however, three new* Chronicle *issues* (Nos. 28, 29, *and* 30), *covering the period of suspension, were handed to Western correspondents in Moscow by Sergei Kovalev and his colleagues in the Initiative Group to Defend Human Rights in the USSR, Tatiana Velikanova and Tatiana Khodorovich. Explaining the resumption of publication, they issued the following statement:*

"Despite the repeated assertion of the KGB and Soviet courts, we do not consider The Chronicle of Current Events

to be an illegal or slanderous publication. We regard it as our duty to promote its widest possible circulation. We are convinced that accurate information about violations of elementary human rights in the Soviet Union should be available to all who are interested."

On December 27, 1974, Kovalev was arrested, and not quite a year later was brought to trial on charges of conducting anti-Soviet agitation and propaganda with subversive intent.

Sakharov and others were barred—throughout the trial's four days—from entering the courtroom. Blocking their path were a number of husky young KGB employees wearing the red armbands of the auxiliary militia, insisting that all the seats inside were taken. In a corner of the lobby stood a well-known KGB colonel conducting what Soviets call "prophylactic work." Spotting a Kovalev sympathizer he knew, the colonel warned him either to leave the courthouse or risk losing his job as a theater fire warden. Even before the trial began, a number of Vilnius Jews had been told that their hitherto unsuccessful applications to emigrate would be reviewed (presumably favorably) if they stayed away from the court. One, Aleksandr Drot, came on the first day anyway, only to have his exit visa delivered to him at home that night with the condition that he promise not to attend any more trial sessions.

From his experience in trying to attend other closed political trials, Sakharov had known what to expect and had anticipated the problems in a letter he wrote in September 1975 to Lev Nikolaevich Smirnov, chairman of the USSR Supreme Court:

I request that you give orders that the trial of Kovalev, which has attracted so much attention in our country and the world, be held in premises large enough to provide sufficient seating for Kovalev's friends (among whom I am honored to count myself) and representatives of the international press and of the organization Amnesty International, to which Kovalev belongs, and without the court's being packed ahead of time by a specially chosen audience, either already prejudiced against the defendant or indifferent to his case. I await your answer.

There was none, but when Sakharov and Kovalev's friends arrived at the courthouse at 8:30 a.m. on December 9, the courtroom doors were closed and the court was filled with spectators, admitted by special pass through a back door. Sakharov went to the third floor of the building, to the office of Judge Ignotas, who was to hear the Kovalev case. Sakharov tried to press a statement into the judge's hands, but, smiling as he hurried out of the room, the judge said: "No, no. I can't accept anything." Sakharov instead left the statement with the judge's office:

I ask that I be called as a witness in the case of Sergei Adamovich Kovalev (Article 70 of the USSR Criminal Code), as I possess important evidence for the court in this case.

Having known Kovalev for many years, I wish to bear witness in this judicial proceeding to his exceptional honesty and conscientiousness, his reverence for law, justice, the defense of human rights and openness. I have expressed my deep respect for S. A. Kovalev by inviting him to be an honored guest at the Nobel ceremony in Oslo, December 10, 1975.

I know that Kovalev is accused of criminal conduct in transmitting materials on political prisoners to foreign correspondents at a press conference on October 30, 1974, of which I was the chairman. In fact, it was I who handed over those materials. I take full responsibility for that action on myself and wish to affirm that fact in court.

I am also the co-author of the letter—introduced as incriminating evidence in the case—to the Chairman of the KGB requesting that the book *The Gulag Archipelago*, by Aleksandr Solzhenitsyn, be returned to Kovalev, its owner.

I ask that this statement of mine be read in court and appended to the file of the case.

P.S. I have also taken part in the composition of many collective declarations and appeals, cited as slanderous in

the charge against S. A. Kovalev. It seems to me incorrect
to use such a term for our joint appeals, and I wish to argue
my point of view before the court.

*The request was denied, but Sakharov did manage that
day to push his way past a shouting KGB colonel and a
secretary into the office of the chairman of the Lithuanian
Supreme Court to register a formal protest against the violation of the law guaranteeing public access to trials. He
did not manage—during the four days of the trial—even to
get a single telephone call through to his wife in Oslo, as the
international operators told him at the Vilnius central post
office either that the large hotel where she was staying did
not answer or that the line was out of order.*

*Meanwhile, the trial proceeded, hearing twenty-two
witnesses called by the prosecution, through two days—as
Sakharov listened to the Voice of America broadcasts from
Oslo of the Nobel ceremonies—to the morning of December
11, when Kovalev for the second time protested the judge's
ordering witnesses out of the room and denying him the
right to call defense witnesses—including those waiting in
the building lobby. Kovalev threatened to continue his hunger strike and abstain from the proceedings if his demands
were not met. They were not. Kovalev was taken from the
courtroom while the prosecutor summed up and called for
a sentence of seven years' imprisonment in a strict-regimen
camp followed by three years of internal exile.*

*That night, Kovalev's friends—fourteen in all, Sakharov
among them—stayed up all night drafting a statement they
telephoned the next morning, December 12, to Moscow to
be passed on to foreign correspondents there. Excerpts follow.*

[Kovalev] is accused of collecting, editing, and disseminating seven issues of the allegedly slanderous *samizdat*
journal, *The Chronicle of Current Events.* . . . To verify
the charge, the investigation tried to examine in detail a few
citations which we will present, since they represent one of
the very few occasions known to us of there being any

analysis at all of the contents of writing alleged to be slanderous.

Chronicle No. 32 had reported that when a search was conducted at the home of the worker Gudas, a Catholic, 2,500 prayerbooks were confiscated, and he was badly beaten. In court Gudas testified to the fact of the confiscation but denied that he had been assaulted.

Chronicle No. 33 listed the names of forty-seven people arrested in Lithuania for their religious convictions. The indictment charges that many of them were actually condemned for their participation in mass murders during the Nazi occupation and for terrorist activities in the postwar period. However, no testimony or witnesses were presented to confirm this charge in court. [In fact, the *Chronicle* had printed the list with a note saying it did not know the specific charges against the prisoners.—Ed.]

The Chronicle of Current Events has given a great deal of attention to psychiatric repression. The court heard testimony from psychiatrists at the Dnepropetrovsk psychiatric hospital, where Leonid Plyushch is held, confirming the official version of his insanity. They tried in their testimony to deny the *Chronicle* account of the poor conditions of his confinement, but contradicted one another on the details. The judge, moreover, refused Kovalev's request to call Plyushch's wife—a major *Chronicle* source—to testify. . . . [Plyushch was released and allowed to emigrate several weeks after the Kovalev trial. Western psychiatrists pronounced him healthy.—Ed.]

At two o'clock in the afternoon of December 12, Kovalev was found guilty on all counts of the indictment and sentenced, as the prosecutor demanded, to seven years in camp and three in exile. Sakharov returned to Moscow, and on December 18, called a press conference to release the following statement:

First of all, I would like to say that Kovalev has been tried for obeying the dictates of his conscience in defending other people who he was firmly convinced had become victims of injustice. The charges against him proved neither that he sought to undermine Soviet power nor that his acts were slanderous. His trial itself was defiantly illegal. It was closed to the public, and the accused was deprived of adversary due process, of the right to defend himself and to make his own closing statement.

Kovalev spent a long time and much effort in preparing a refutation of the charges, especially those which related to *The Chronicle of Current Events.* The seven issues of the *Chronicle* which were held to incriminate him reported on 694 incidents. The charges were based on 172 of them. Kovalev did not exclude possibility of error in eleven instances, but intended to prove that none of these errors could be characterized as intentionally defamatory. Even the investigators agreed that eighty-nine reports were accurate, and Kovalev intended to prove that there was no error in the seventy-two other *Chronicle* reports. He was denied any chance, however, even to begin to carry out this task. Doubtless it will be a long time before we are able to know his well-thought-out and convincing arguments.

At the trial, the prosecution tried to use seven incidents to prove the charge of slander. Today we can assert that only in one or two insignificant cases could the charges cast doubt on the accuracy of the *Chronicle* reports.

The arrest and conviction of Kovalev is a challenge to Soviet and world public opinion. After Helsinki and during the Nobel ceremony, the authorities clearly wanted to make a stubborn show of strength, even at the expense of making a travesty of their own laws. To allow this challenge to go unanswered would be to betray both an outstanding person and those central principles on which so much depends. The only possible response is to demand the reversal of the sentence against Kovalev.

The sentence, however, was upheld, and within a year Sakharov's concern for Kovalev was focused on his friend's health. On October 31, 1976, Sakharov wrote for the second time to the Minister of Internal Affairs, appealing for the prisoner's transfer to a Leningrad prison hospital so that he might have a needed operation. He received no answer,

*and reports from the Perm prison indicated that Kovalev
was being subjected to continual harassment. Out of his
first year in camp Kovalev spent a total of nearly a month
in punishment cells.*

In an interview with a Newsweek *correspondent on
February 24, 1977, Sakharov explained the ties between
détente and human rights, using the Kovalev case as a
specific example:*

Q: How effective is the influence of world public
opinion? Is it sufficient? Or should the West use other
measures—refuse to trade in grain, restrict credits, delay
disarmament agreements—until the USSR begins to observe
the human rights provisions of the Helsinki agreements?

A: Statements in defense of human rights in the USSR
and in the countries of Eastern Europe are important always
and everywhere. The fact that violations of these rights
continue underlines the necessity for a long-term, persistent
and patient struggle using a widening range of methods,
including different techniques of exerting pressure. Let
me give you an example to illustrate that persistence is
essential.

In the summer of 1976, the Federation of American
Scientists wrote a letter of appeal to the Soviet Minister of
Internal Affairs, Shchelokov, with a request that Kovalev
be transferred to a prison hospital in Leningrad for examination and an operation. The Federation never received a
response and, as far as I know, did not react in any way to
this violation of generally accepted norms of international
behavior. Now Kovalev's situation is even worse than half
a year ago.

Under these circumstances, I would consider it acceptable to apply pressure through a partial boycott of scientific and cultural contacts or a partial cutback in the supply
of certain types of technology. I would not, however, ap-
prove such measures as a total refusal to allocate credits,
a refusal to sell grain, or a refusal to confer on disarmament.
*We must not forget that only détente created the possibility
of exerting even minimal influence on both the domestic
and foreign policies of the Socialist countries. In the name*

of détente they are required to accommodate their actions to universal humanitarian standards. It would be a great misfortune to return to the past. [Emphasis added.—Ed.]

I consider the use of food aid for political purposes morally unacceptable. And it is absolutely unacceptable— even for a goal as important as respect for human rights— to make conduct in that area a precondition for disarmament negotiations. Disarmament must have first priority.

Let me repeat emphatically, though, that legislative measures such as the Jackson-Vanik Amendment addressed to the defense of human rights and separate from other aspects of détente are extremely important and justified. That is an example of a moral approach to political problems, in accord with the moral principles of American democracy. Greater unity among the countries of the West is essential for the complete success of such legislative measures.

In Kovalev's case, Sakharov's persistence—including his mentioning Kovalev at the top of his list of Soviet prisoners in a letter to President Carter (see Chapter IV)—and Western support did bring some positive results. Within a week after his comment to the Newsweek *correspondent, Sakharov learned that Kovalev—who had been on a protest hunger strike since early February when prison camp authorities cut short the visit he was entitled to have with his wife and son—had been transferred to the Leningrad prison hospital. Sakharov wrote a letter of gratitude, March 2, 1977, to A. M. Rosenthal, editor of* The New York Times:

Through your paper I want to thank everyone in America, Europe and the Soviet Union who helped to effect the transfer of my very ill friend, Sergei Kovalev, from a Perm camp to the Leningrad prison hospital, thereby possibly saving his life.

Andrei Sakharov
Nobel Peace Prize Laureate

Kovalev's own resolute conduct certainly played a role in the transfer. Even after it, he continued his fast until March 11, thirty-five days in all, reducing his weight to

117 pounds. On March 24, he was permitted the meeting he had fought to obtain with his wife, and the next day he was successfully operated on. No malignancy—which camp doctors had suspected—was found, and by April 15, Sergei Kovalev had been sent back to his prison camp beyond the Urals. There, after the hospitalization, he had about a half-year of comparatively "peaceful" camp life.

In the fall of 1977 he renounced the right to correspond after the post office "lost" five of his letters (his entire allowance for a two-month period) in a row, all of which had already been passed by the camp censor. And in May 1978 he was confined to an internal camp prison for a six-month term for "systematic disregard of administrative regulations and purposeful failure to fulfill the work norms." Kovalev performed "only" 86 percent of his required workload.

III

For Freedom, Against Persecution

The following appeal to the Conference of European Communist Parties, held in East Berlin after protracted dickering between Kremlin loyalists and Romanian, Yugoslav, French, Italian, and Spanish party officials over the subordination to or autonomy from Moscow of the Eurocommunists, was signed and sent from Moscow, June 28, 1976, by Sakharov, Valentin Turchin, and Professor Yuri Orlov.†

Turchin, a computer scientist forced to emigrate in 1977, had been a public supporter of Sakharov since 1973, when Turchin and others also established the Moscow branch of Amnesty International. A distinguished physicist, Orlov founded the Soviet Helsinki Watch Group in May 1976, and was its active head until his arrest in February 1977. After a four-day closed trial he was sentenced on May 18, 1978, to seven years' imprisonment and five years' internal exile for anti-Soviet agitation and propaganda.

Distinguished delegates to the Conference of European Communist Parties:

We propose that you put the problem of human rights in Communist countries on the Conference's agenda and that you also determine your general position of principle on this issue. The need to observe the fundamental human rights enunciated in the United Nations' Universal Declaration of Human Rights and established in part by the International Human Rights Covenants is now widely accepted.

The leaders of the Communist parties of Europe have repeatedly declared their adherence to the idea of human rights and democratic forms of government. One can only welcome these declarations.

It is clear, however, that people do and will continue to judge the theory and practice of Communist parties by the conditions in countries where Communists are in power, above all by conditions in the Soviet Union. Although the situation in our country has radically improved in comparison to the Stalinist period, it is still characterized by the systematic and widespread violation of individuals' elementary civil and political rights, by undemocratic forms of government, and by the arbitrary rule of the authorities.

We would especially like to draw your attention to two aspects of this problem.

1. On the policies of the CPSU° toward civic organizations   Article 126 of the Constitution of the USSR [of 1936—Ed.] provides that the leadership of all civil associations should be formed by the Communist Party of the Soviet Union. This provision gives the authorities the formal grounds to declare unconstitutional any public organization established and administered without the sanction of party and governmental organs. In particular, this restriction applies to cultural and humanitarian organizations like the Initiative Group to Defend Human Rights, the Soviet chapter of Amnesty International, the Public Groups to Promote Observance of the Helsinki Agreement in the USSR [Helsinki Watch—Ed.], the Council of Relatives of Evangelical Christian-Baptist Prisoners, and others.

In view of this, we request answers to the following specific questions:

How does the Conference regard the party policy described above? Do you not see it as a violation of a fundamental civil right?

Is the existence of independent public organizations

° Communist Party of the Soviet Union.

possible in a Communist state? If so, what kind? What limitations on public organizations are permissible in a Communist country? How does the Conference view the creation of independent cultural and humanitarian organizations in the USSR, particularly those listed above? Do you consider repression of citizens participating in such organizations justified?

2. On the right to exchange information, freedom of thought and conscience Articles 70 and 190.1 of the Criminal Code of the RSFSR° and the matching laws in other Union Republics provide long prison sentences for the dissemination of slanderous fabrications defaming the state and social system. These laws are used to send people to prisons, labor camps, and psychiatric hospitals for the simple exchange of information, for expressing ideas unsanctioned by the CPSU, and for reading and possessing books and manuscripts not approved by the authorities. Specifically, people are persecuted for distributing information journals such as *The Chronicle of Current Events, The Fraternal Newsletter of the Council of Evangelical Christian-Baptist Churches, The Chronicle of the Lithuanian Catholic Church,* and others.

We ask the Conference to discuss and answer the following questions.

What kinds of guarantees should be provided for the freedom to exchange information and the freedom of thought and conscience in countries governed by Communist parties? What kinds of guarantees for an independent juridical-legal system should there be in these states? Does the Conference not find that the absence of an independent press in the USSR attests to the absence of free speech? Does the Conference consider the repression of people for distributing *samizdat* information bulletins and other journals, especially *The Chronicle of Current Events,* to be

---

° Russian Soviet Federated Socialist Republic.

justified? What is the Conference's attitude toward the sentencing of Sergei Kovalev to seven years in prison and three years in exile? How does the Conference view other political trials which have been the subject of widespread attention in the past few months? Particularly, what is the Conference's judgment on the trial of members of the Estonian Democratic Movement, as well as the trials of Vladimir Osipov,† Mustafa Dzhemilev, and the secretary of the Soviet branch of Amnesty International, Andrei Tverdokhlebov?

In appealing to the Conference of leaders of Communist parties, we believe it necessary to repeat anew the call for an amnesty of all political prisoners.

In the October 1975 trial of the Estonian Democratic Movement, the Estonian SSR Supreme Court sentenced Sergei Soldatov† and Kalya Myattik to six years and Mati Kiirend† and Artem Jushkevich to five years in strict-regimen camps. As reported in issue No. 38 of The Chronicle of Current Events: *"The accused were charged with compiling, reproducing, and distributing more than forty documents, in particular, 'Programs of the Estonian Democratic Movement'; 'Programs of the Estonian National Front'; the journals* Estonian Democrat *and* The Estonian National Voice, *in Estonian; the journals* Democrat *and* The Ray of Freedom, *in Russian; 'A Memorandum to the UN General Assembly'; 'A Letter to UN Secretary General Kurt Waldheim' . . ."*

Vladimir Osipov, editor of the samizdat *journal* Veche, *was sentenced in September 1975 to eight years in a strict-regimen camp, his second sentence under Article 70.* Veche *was the medieval Russian term for a people's assembly, and the nine issues of the review edited by Ospiov were notable for their emphasis on Russian culture and national themes.*

Mustafa Dzhemilev (Abduldzhemil) was born in 1943 and in 1944 was deported from the Crimea along with the rest of his people. He is one of the leaders of the movement of Crimean Tatars to return to their homeland. In 1966, he

*was expelled from school for his participation in the move-
ment, and, for refusing to serve in the army, was sentenced
to one and a half years' imprisonment. He became a member of the Initiative Group to Defend Human Rights in the
USSR in 1969. In 1970, he was sentenced under Article
190.1 to three years' imprisonment on a charge of "circulating fabrications known to be false which defame the Soviet state and social system," and in 1974, for refusing to
report for military induction, he was again sentenced to a
year's incarceration. Three days before his scheduled release,
however, he was transferred from camp to the Omsk prison
in connection with a new slander charge. While awaiting
trial in prison, he went on an eight-month hunger strike in
protest, but was sentenced in April 1976 to two and a half
years in a strict-regimen camp. The verdict was based on
evidence given to the pretrial investigation by Dzhemilev's
cellmate, Vladimir Dvoryansky, even though at the trial,
Dvoryansky recanted his testimony and said he had been
pressured into giving evidence by threats against him and
his family and by promises that his own prison-camp term
would be reduced. Dvoryansky was subsequently convicted
of perjury for recanting his pretrial evidence. The Dzhemilev decision was also based on several of the Tatar spokesman's letters and one statement he had drafted: "Declaration of Principles of the Crimean Tatar Movement." Three
copies of this declaration in English, Tatar, and Arabic were
taken from Dzhemilev during a search of his cell, and the
court concluded that Dzhemilev had written them with the
aim of circulating them.*

*The physicist Andrei Tverdokhlebov was a founding
member of the Moscow Human Rights Committee. After a
year in prison awaiting trial, he was sentenced in April
1976 to five years in exile—reduced, since each day in pretrial prison detention counts as three days of exile—which
he served in the village of Nyurbachan in the Komi Autono-
mous Republic until his release in January 1978. He was
charged with being the author of the pamphlet* On the Conditions of Political Prisoners, *and several letters (including
a letter to the International League for Human Rights and*

a letter to the President of South Vietnam calling for the release of South Vietnamese political prisoners). He was also accused of joining in collective appeals and of distributing articles by Sakharov and Aleksandr Solzhenitsyn.

On September 25, 1976, Sakharov sent the following address to a meeting of the International League for Human Rights:

I am very grateful for the honor you have shown me by electing me an honorary vice-president of the International League of Human Rights. I share with everyone gathered in this hall the basic principle that lies at the heart of the League's work—the priority of human rights among the problems facing mankind.

I hope that in spite of the difficulties facing the campaign in defense of human rights in the USSR, I shall be able to work closely with the League. However, such collaboration will be possible only if the blockade of my international mail and telephone communications, which the Soviet authorities have imposed (with brief interruptions) for two years now, is lifted.

Today, I will not talk about all the political prisoners in the USSR—those who have been sentenced for religious activities, for attempting to leave the country, for reading and possessing officially unsanctioned literature, those who have been charged with so-called "nationalism," and others. I would rather remind this body of the fate of those whose work has been devoted to defending human rights of others, those who have engaged in collecting and distributing information on human-rights violations in the USSR. These are not political activists. They have no expectation that their work can or will change the political structure of our country. They seek no personal reward. On the contrary, their work makes their lives and the lives of those close to them incredibly difficult, often wretched. Nevertheless, they look on the suffering of each innocently convicted person as their own personal misfortune.

They are men like Sergei Kovalev, Andrei Tverdokhlebov, Vladimir Bukovsky,† Semyon Gluzman,† Kronid Lyubarsky,† Gabriel Superfin,† Viktor Khaustov,† and Anatoly Marchenko.† Their commitment and their activity gave birth to the civic awareness of human-rights issues in our country. The health and lives of many of these men are now in danger from the hunger, cold, often unendurable labor, and other hardships in the camps and in exile. Detailed information on the situation of each of these men can be drawn from the publications of Amnesty International, Khronika Press, and others.

I am convinced that under these conditions—when activities in defense of human rights are cruelly repressed in a whole series of countries—our duty, the duty of the League, is to protect the freedom and the lives of our friends and comrades in the fight for human rights throughout the world.

Anatoly Marchenko, mentioned by Sakharov above, first expressed his dissent by attempting to flee from the Soviet Union to Iran in 1960. Another Soviet who attempted to escape to Iran—16 years after Marchenko—was Valentin Zosimov. He succeeded in crossing the border in a light plane in October 1976, but was handed back to Soviet authorities almost immediately. In a letter they wrote on October 29, 1976, to the Shah of Iran and U.S. President Ford—and handed in to an Iranian consul in Moscow five days later—Sakharov and Elena Bonner, his wife, called for international efforts to save Zosimov:

It was with horror that we learned that Valentin Zosimov, the pilot who flew to Iran and requested asylum in the United States, has been turned over to Soviet authorities. We are certain that you cannot help but feel your responsibility for the fate of this man. He had counted on humane treatment and the international right to asylum.

The absence of a guaranteed right to emigration pushed Zosimov to this desperate step, as it had many before him: those who have perished over the years trying to cross the frontiers of the Soviet Union; those who have died at the Berlin Wall; Simas Kudirka, the Lithuanian sailor handed back by American seamen; the Jews convicted in Leningrad in 1970.

We remember the last two incidents particularly well. The return of Kudirka was a national disgrace for the U.S., and only the subsequent, persistent efforts of the American authorities removed the stain. The Leningrad affair clearly revealed the ominous features of Soviet justice which now threaten Zosimov. In similar trials, "flight across the border" has been characterized as "treason," although this charge defies logic and even other articles of the Criminal Code. It was on these grounds that the major defendants in the Leningrad trial were sentenced to death; only the intercession of world public opinion saved their lives.

Zosimov has not committed treason; he has brought no harm to the USSR. He committed no acts of air piracy, for his actions endangered no one's life. We fear, however, that he could be sentenced to death at a closed trial without anyone knowing.

We call on you, your highness, and you, Mr. President, to use all your influence to save the life of Valentin Zosimov.

According to reports, Zosimov was not sentenced to death but imprisoned in Camp 37 of the Perm political prison-camp complex, indicating that he, like Kudirka and the defendants of the 1970 Leningrad hijacking trial, had been convicted under Article 64 of the RSFSR Criminal Code (treason).

In October 1970, Simas Kudirka jumped from a Soviet fishing trawler to an American Coast Guard ship, the Vigilant. *Soviet sailors were permitted to board the* Vigilant *and take Kudirka back by force. He was sentenced to ten years in a strict-regimen labor camp. In the summer of 1974, however, he was declared a citizen of the United States (his mother had been born in the United States but "acquired" Soviet citizenship after the takeover of Lithu-*

*ania), and was pardoned that August and given permission
to emigrate to the United States.*

*The same day that he wrote the appeal for Zosimov,
Sakharov put down the following short plea—to be read a
month later at an Amnesty International meeting in London
on political prisoners—for ten named "prisoners of conscience" and for the general amnesty he has long advocated:*

I call on you to raise your voices in defense of prisoners
of conscience. Their suffering, their courageous, nonviolent
struggle for the noble principles of justice, openness, com-
passion, human and national dignity, and freedom of conscience, obligate us all not to forget them and to obtain
their release from the cruel clutch of the punitive apparatus.

I will cite only a few of the better-known prisoners of
conscience in my country, behind each of whom stand many
more. They are Vladimir Bukovsky, Semyon Gluzman, Sergei Kovalev, Mustafa Dzhemilev, Valentin Moroz,† Petras
Paulaitis,† Georgy Vins,† Vasily Romanyuk,† Danilo Shumuk,† and Paruir Airikian.† My friends at this meeting can
tell you about their lives and achievements, but what I wish
to stress is the tragic situation of each of them.

I call you to the fight for freedom for each of the political prisoners whose names are known to you, for the release
of all political prisoners in the USSR, Eastern Europe, and
the entire world.

I call for a general amnesty of political prisoners!

*Also, on October 29, Sakharov sent British Prime Minis-
ter James Callaghan a special appeal for one of the best-
known prisoners of conscience, Vladimir Bukovsky:*

Esteemed Mr. Callaghan:

I appeal to you to support the campaign, begun in Eng-
land and many other countries, to defend the Soviet political prisoner Vladimir Bukovsky.

He was sentenced to seven years' imprisonment and five years' exile for his courageous defense of the victims of psychiatric repression. Now, ill and exhausted, he is serving his sentence in Vladimir Prison, a place notorious for its barbaric conditions, for the torture of its dank punishment cells, for the unbearable cold and hunger and the stifling seals on the windows of its airless cubicles.

Bukovsky's fate, his noble, nonviolent struggle, binds him to hundreds of other prisoners of conscience in the USSR—Kovalev, Gluzman, Dzhemilev, Vins, Romanyuk, Shumuk, and others. In fighting for Bukovsky's release, we are fighting for all of them.

In this age of détente, there has come a great increase in both the right and the opportunity to intercede whenever and wherever human rights—freedom of belief, of movement, and of information flow—are violated. At the same time, and in the same measure, the international danger from human-rights violations and the universal responsibility for such violations are likewise growing. The opportunities and obligations are particularly great for government leaders engaged in diplomatic meetings, for, in the course of such contacts, any mention of a specific name or a specific violation can have decisive impact.

In appealing to you today, I rely on your compassionate understanding and active support in the struggle to free Vladimir Bukovsky and other political prisoners in the USSR, the countries of Eastern Europe, and the whole world.

The next day, October 30, Sakharov handed an American correspondent in Moscow written answers to questions about the position of Soviet political prisoners. From that "interview" (which was never published in America, though parts of it appeared in the Norwegian press) comes the following exchange:

Q: The Soviet regime says that the dissenters Sergei Kovalev and Andrei Tverdokhlebov were convicted because they had violated Soviet law. Can you say something about Soviet legality?

A: What the Soviet legal system, as a whole, lacks is the tradition of impartiality, judicial independence, and the pursuit of justice as an abstract concept. This is apparent not only in its treatment of dissenters. I receive hundreds of desperate letters from people convicted in common criminal (not political) cases and from their relatives. Even allowing for the partiality and prejudice of my correspondents, I still cannot help but be filled with horror at the picture they describe. It is one of judicial tyranny and corruption, of cruelty and the absence of any willingness of those in authority to right wrongs or injustices. Without bothering to collect real evidence, investigators (either themselves or with the help of other prisoners) often beat the required confession out of the accused. I read about such occurrences in almost every letter I receive. In Kazakhstan, a nineteen-year-old boy, Igor Brusnikin,† died this way. Fortunately, we do not hear of such behavior now in political cases.

Some courts consider even the most serious cases, such as premeditated murder, which carries a death penalty, in an exceptionally superficial manner, ignoring all contradictory evidence and defense requests. The case of Rafkat Shaimukhamedov,† a Tatar worker who was executed by a firing squad in January 1976, after two years on death row, is a frightening example of the way our judicial apparatus sometimes works mercilessly and unjustly. (The prosecutor, and apparently the "author," of this case was Bekboev.)

Let's say a political case comes before *this kind* of court —a case in which the sentence has already been decided at high levels of the KGB. The members of the court know very well that any "free thinking" they might show would only harm their careers. Disguised KGB agents zealously guard the courtroom itself against any unapproved observers of this judicial farce. Can you expect a fair verdict under these conditions?

Kovalev and Tverdokhlebov, as many before them, were convicted under Articles 70 and 190.1 of the RSFSR Criminal Code. The concepts contained in these laws—anti-Soviet agitation and propaganda, slanderous fabrications, the presence of an intent to subvert or weaken the

Soviet state and social system—have never been juridically defined. The falsity of the statements or publications which are cited to incriminate the accused cannot be proved by the courts simply because such documents talk about the very human-rights violations which are so common in our country. As a result, we get pure demagoguery—you see it confirmed in articles in the Soviet press reporting that Kovalev and Tverdokhlebov were convicted not for their beliefs, but for "specific criminal acts of slander."

Proving the existence of an intent to subvert the Soviet system is equally difficult. The goals of the nonviolent struggle for human rights, for free discussion and justice, for the openness of Soviet society, are not subversive, but constructive; not political, but humane and civic. All mankind has a stake in the realization of these goals.

In the same October 30 "interview," Sakharov spoke of other political hardship cases and—a constant preoccupation—of the lack of coherence in the West's efforts to influence Soviet conduct:

Q: In your opinion, does Western public opinion have a greater influence on the Soviet Union now than in the past?

A: The expansion of contacts with the West—economic, technical, scientific, and cultural—opens up a whole range of possibilities. However, we see in practice that despite the appeals by thousands for the release of Bukovsky, Vins, Moroz, Gluzman, Sergienko,† Kuznetsov,† Shtern,† and other political prisoners, and for permission for Slepak, Lerner, and Levich to emigrate, the Soviet authorities persist in their refusals.

Apparently, the effectiveness of these campaigns is lessened by inadequate coordination in organizing them. More important, however, there is not enough involvement by those people and organizations who maintain direct contacts with the USSR—specifically, governmental and legislative bodies, business groups, and scientific, technological, and cultural organizations. I am convinced that it is absolutely essential to unite these forces and that their unity will produce concrete results.

Aside from his intercessions on behalf of individuals, Sakharov has long campaigned for a general amnesty for prisoners convicted of nonviolent political offenses. Amnesties are often promulgated in the Soviet Union on the occasion of major national celebrations—the anniversary of the 1917 Revolution or of the end of World War II, for example—and just before the November 1977 observance of the Revolution's sixtieth anniversary, Sakharov, General Grigorenko,† and thirty-eight others joined in a plea to the Presidium of the Supreme Soviet to extend the expected amnesty decree to political prisoners.

On November 5, the decree was published, providing, according to a TASS dispatch, for amnesty to those serving sentences up to five years who had seen combat defending the USSR, or had once received Soviet orders or medals, or were women or minors. Additionally, men over sixty, women over fifty-five, mothers of underage children, pregnant women, and disabled persons were pardoned. Amnesty was specifically denied, however, to particularly dangerous recidivists, those convicted of grave crimes, and persons "convicted for particularly dangerous offenses against the state." The exclusion covered all the dissenters (except one woman in exile) for whom Sakharov had campaigned, and, disappointed, he released the following statement:

I am heartened by the release of several thousand people from the camps and prisons. The living conditions and forced labor in Soviet penal institutions are extraordinarily difficult, and I am gladdened by the amnesty, an act that is always one of mercy.

Unfortunately, today's amnesty, like those that have preceded it, is unjustifiably restrictive in its effect on all categories of prisoners. It is especially narrow in the authority it gives penal officials to make their evaluation of a prisoner's conduct a criterion for granting or denying amnesty. It seems, in fact, that the amnesty decree was designed to preclude any significant decline in the work force for construction sites and factories in the far east and north.

I am deeply disappointed that the amnesty excludes prisoners of conscience, those who suffer without having committed any crime. These people rejected violence to choose free and open speech as their only weapon. They are suffering for their defense of human rights, their pursuit of openness, and their religious activity.

The failure to mention inmates of psychiatric hospitals or those convicted for attempting to leave a country that blocks legal emigration is likewise disillusioning. And I am distressed that there was no decree eliminating the death sentence, an act which would have been important and humane.

The persecution of prisoners of conscience in the USSR is a challenge to world public opinion. I am certain that sooner or later justice and reason will triumph.

The year that ended in such disappointment had begun with hope, much of it based on anticipation of a vigorous Western human-rights policy under the leadership of the newly elected American President, Jimmy Carter. Sakharov had welcomed Carter's election and, even before he was inaugurated, was pleading with him to intercede in a particularly repellent miscarriage of Soviet justice.

The case involved a completely unknown Ukrainian woodworker, Pyotr Vasilevich Ruban. He was sentenced in the Chernigov Oblast Court on December 29, 1976, to eight years in camp and five in exile for theft of government property in especially large amounts and for engaging in private enterprise. Ruban, whose previous five-year prison-camp term, apparently for his nationalist views, had ended in 1973, had made a trinket commemorating the U.S. Bicentennial—a wooden bookcover inlaid with a design of the Statue of Liberty—which had been stolen from his workshop. After the theft Ruban was himself arrested, charged, and convicted of a crime similar to embezzlement—for having used what the court held were wood chips worth 772 rubles (roughly equal to an average Soviet worker's salary for five months) to make souvenirs for sale through a state-owned shop.

Even Soviet courts found the conviction hard to swallow. The first trial was overturned on appeal, but at a new one, lasting seven days and ending on April 20, 1977, Ruban was found guilty of a completely different charge— anti-Soviet agitation—based on remarks he had made in the diary he kept while serving his first sentence. Ruban identified the cause of his persecution in a statement to the court: "I am being tried because I wanted the Ukraine to secede from the USSR, because I served five years for that and did not change my views."

He was found guilty, but got a slightly shorter sentence from the second trial: six years' imprisonment and three years in exile. It is unusual—though not unheard of— for Soviet courts to review an ordinary criminal case, but exceedingly rare to review a political proceeding. It is logical to suspect that the publicity given Ruban's case in the West was part of the political motive for the "legal" action.

Part of that publicity was the telegram Andrei Sakharov sent to President-elect Jimmy Carter on January 3, 1977:

The artist Pyotr Ruban has been sentenced to eight years in prison camp and five years in exile on a trumped-up charge. The real reason is that he made a souvenir as a gift to the American people on the 200th anniversary of their independence: a wooden bookcover inlaid with a design of the Statue of Liberty. I call on you to defend Pyotr Ruban in the name of friendship between the common people of our countries—the only real guarantee of peace.

IV

The Carter Correspondence

The Sakharov telegram to President-elect Carter about Pyotr Ruban was only one episode in what was to become a major political test for the new American Administration. From his Inaugural Address pledge not to be "indifferent to the fate of freedom elsewhere," the President was committed to a policy course Sakharov had urged during the campaign and welcomed in practice. Washington commentators and even the President's advisers were, however, divided over the wisdom of the Carter human-rights posture and particularly over how it should be implemented. Few wanted to make the Soviet Union either the first target of the campaign or the test of the policy's efficacy. As the material in this chapter shows, events—many of them accidents—brought the question of Soviet human-rights performance to an early prominence. In effect, Sakharov forced the Administration to a quick decision on what was and remains an explosive East-West issue.

Sakharov's efforts began during the Presidential campaign itself with the following appeal to the incumbent, Gerald Ford, and his challenger, Jimmy Carter. It was sent from Moscow on October 11, 1976, and signed "with profound respect and hope, Andrei Sakharov, Nobel Peace Prize Laureate":

Now that the candidates are campaigning for the American Presidency and preparing and presenting to the American people the principles of their future policies, I consider it important once again to express publicly certain positions which I view as having primary significance.

I am convinced that guaranteed political and civil rights for people the world over are also guarantees of international security, economic and social progress, and environmental protection. Freedom of belief and conscience, free exchange of information, freedom of movement, and the freedom to choose one's country of residence—such rights cannot be set apart from the basic problems facing mankind. And in the defense of human rights there can be no place for isolationism or national self-seeking.

By broadening the recognition of these principles, the Helsinki declaration has opened new possibilities for international action. Among them is the campaign for a general, worldwide amnesty for political prisoners. You know that in our country and in other countries of Eastern Europe, in China, and in many countries of the Third World and the West, there are now thousands of prisoners of conscience in prisons, camps, and special psychiatric hospitals, condemned for their participation in the exchange of information, for their beliefs, for religious activity, for an attempt to leave the country. They are undergoing cold, hunger, backbreaking toil, persecutions, and humiliations which are unworthy of the civilized world. I call upon you not to lessen your efforts in the struggle for the freedom to choose one's country of residence. I stress again the exceptional importance of the free international flow of people and information, including unhindered radio broadcasting.

It is my hope that in the spirit of the freedom-loving and humane tradition of the American people, the commitment to advance human rights throughout the world will occupy an ever greater place in U.S. policy.

The day after Jimmy Carter won the election, Sakharov sent him a short but fervent telegram of congratulations:

I welcome your election. Your decisive unambiguous statements in defense of human rights throughout the world are of vast significance. They raise new hopes. I am sure that the USA—full of courage and determination, strong in its democratic and moral traditions, powerful in its economic and military resources, the first country of the West—will carry with honor the burden history has placed upon her citizens and leaders.

On January 21, when a member of Moscow's community of Jewish "refuseniks"—those, like Benjamin Levich, Aleksandr Lerner, and Vladimir Slepak, denied permission to emigrate to Israel—brought an American lawyer, Martin Garbus, and his wife to the Sakharov apartment, the Soviet physicist was in an anxious frame of mind. Twice since a bomb had exploded in the Moscow subway on January 8, he had spoken out forcefully to warn that the KGB might use the explosion as a pretext for new repression against dissidents. But sensationalistic hints that the nonviolent dissenters might be turning in frustration to terrorism were receiving more attention in the West than Sakharov's and others' vigorous denials that any such thing had occurred or could.

Thus when Garbus suggested that he could carry a letter from Sakharov to President Carter, Sakharov responded eagerly to the proposal. Garbus had come to Moscow to speak to Soviet officials about the conviction of Amner Zavurov, a young "refusednik" in Uzbekistan caught in a Catch-22 prosecution for not having the internal passport authorities had taken from him when they gave him permission to emigrate. Now Garbus had only an hour or two before his flight back to America. Sakharov normally requires half a dozen or more drafts before writing the final version of any statement. This time, however, he wrote hurriedly, and Garbus' "refusednik" escort produced an equally hasty English translation on the spot. The resulting versions do not always match in paragraph order or even in content. The Russian original, for instance, listed only fifteen names of prisoners on whose behalf Sakharov appealed to the President, but the names of Gabriel Superfin† and Vasily Fedorenko† appear in the English translation, suggesting the unusual hurry with which the letter was composed.

*A week after the Moscow meeting, Garbus gave Sak-
harov's letter to State Department officials and to reporters
for* The New York Times *and* Los Angeles Times. *A letter
the author had intended as a private communication sud-
denly became a public event, printed January 29 in a
slightly abbreviated version in a major U.S. paper just as
Americans were beginning to understand the seriousness
and the complexity of Jimmy Carter's commitment to human rights. The letter itself—in an edited text combining
the Russian original and the English translation done in
Moscow—follows:*

Dear Mr. Carter,

It's very important to defend those who suffer because
of their nonviolent struggle for an open society, for justice,
for other people whose rights are violated. It is our duty and
yours to fight for them. I think that a lot depends on this
struggle—trust between peoples, confidence in lofty promises, and, in the final analysis, international security.

Our situation is difficult, almost unbearable—not only
in the USSR, but also in all the countries of Eastern Europe.
Now, on the eve of the Belgrade Meeting, with the struggle
for human rights rising in Eastern Europe and the USSR,
the authorities are stepping up their repression and their
attempts to discredit dissidents. They are unwilling to make
any concessions to the human rights most essential to any
society (freedom of belief and information, freedom of conscience, freedom to choose one's country of residence, etc.).
They cannot accept the honest competition of ideas. The
persecution of the members of the Helsinki Watch Groups
in Moscow and the Ukraine, and especially the provocation
in the Moscow subway, which we have to compare to the
1933 Reichstag fire and the 1934 murder of Kirov, require
emphatic condemnation.

Do you know the truth about the situation of religion
in the USSR—the humiliation of official churches and the
merciless repression (arrests; fines; religious parents deprived of their children; even murder, as in the case of the
Baptist Biblenko†) of those sects—Baptists, Uniates, Pente-

costals, the True Orthodox Church, and others—who seek independence of the government. The Vins† case is the best-known example. Terror is also used against other groups of dissidents. During the past year we have known of the murders of dissidents—that of the poet and translator Konstantin Bogatyrev† is well known—which have not been investigated at all.

It is very important that the President of the United States continue his efforts to obtain the release of those people who are already known to Americans and that those efforts not be in vain. It is very important to continue the struggle for the severely ill and for women political prisoners.

I give you a list of those in need of immediate release, but it is very important to remember that there are many others in equally difficult situations. This is the main list. There are very many others who need the same support, and we haven't got the moral·strength to cross out any of the names: Kovalev, Romanyuk,† Dzhemilev, Svitlichny,† Gluzman,† Ruban, Shtern,† Yuri Fyodorov,† Makarenko,† Sergienko,† Ogurtsov,† Pronyuk,† Maria Semyonova,† Vins,† Moroz,† Superfin,† Fedorenko.† (Fedorenko has been on a hunger strike for two years. He is serving a thirteen-year sentence for high treason since he tried to cross the frontier by hanging to the undercarriage of a train.) Detailed information about each of them is available from Khronika Press; its publisher, Edward Kline, knows all the cases.

I have a serious problem with communications. My telephone to the West is completely blocked. No calls reach me, and it is useless to go to the telephone station [in the post office—Ed.] since I'm always told that the other party doesn't answer. (I'm always closely watched.) This question of communications is basic to my public activity and the entire human-rights movement in this country. I ask you to take steps at the international level in this connection.

I also want to ask especially that you raise your voice in defense of [Yugoslav writer] Mihajlo Mihajlov,   the

Charter '77 group in Czechoslovakia, and the Workers'
Defense Committee in Poland. With profound respect,

Andrei Sakharov

On February 2, Sakharov told a Newsweek *interviewer
that he had not meant his letter to President Carter to be
public. The exchange:*

Q: Are you disappointed that your appeal to President
Carter was published? Can the West achieve more through
quiet diplomacy than by public statements?

A: The first and second parts of your question relate
to completely different themes. I attach great importance
to publicity, and I am convinced that the defense of human
rights is impossible unless the world knows about violations
of these rights. As I have already said, however, I do not
think I have the right to give any advice or recommendations about what specific measures should be taken by officials in foreign countries.

In regard to my letter to Mr. Carter, it was written
during an American lawyer's visit which lasted less than
one hour because he was rushing to catch his plane. This
was not an appeal which I had intended to be made public.
I do not know why *The New York Times* decided to print
it. Yet, if the publication of this letter helps even one of
the seventeen people mentioned in the letter, then I will
be completely satisfied.

*Interviewed for CBS on February 10, Sakharov urged
Washington to be firm on human rights:*

Q: What do you see as the attitude of the Carter Administration to you and to other dissidents? Do you think
that Washington policies have an effect? What should the
Carter Administration say or do?

A: The new President's moral, courageous position
evokes my respect and hope. It is not interference in other
countries' internal affairs to conduct a decisive, consistent,
and principled defense of human rights throughout the

world. On the contrary, such conduct preserves the moral, democratic values of the American people and of mankind as a whole. It is the preservation of a free future for the United States and for the entire world.

I have neither the right nor the opportunity to give advice to the new Administration about how it should act in any particular situation. I can only permit myself to say that any disagreement, uncertainty, or partial retreat will give the Soviet authorities the impression that the new administration is giving in to blackmail and pressure. I am deeply convinced that will not actually occur, for any appearance of weakness will affect all aspects of East-West relations, including disarmament negotiations. Unfortunately, the recent episode of the statement issued by the State Department after I was called in by the Procuracy did give Soviet authorities just such a misleading impression of the new Administration's weakness or vacillation. Possibly this is one of the reasons for the wave of repressions in recent days, although it is perfectly clear that these repressions were planned before this. I repeat, I am absolutely convinced that the Soviet authorities have a false impression. The most recent declarations by the President and by the Secretary of State support my belief and hope.

I have often spoken of the key importance of the problem of the choice of one's country of residence. Carter's telegram to Vladimir Slepak during the presidential campaign shows that the President shares that opinion. It gives me hope that this issue will remain part of the President's unwavering concern.

The "episode" of a State Department declaration on Sakharov which Secretary of State Cyrus Vance had not cleared for release caused great comment in the Washington press and some real anxiety for Sakharov in Moscow. It is discussed in detail in Chapter VI.

The "repressions" referred to were the arrests of Helsinki Watchers Mykola Rudenko† and Oleksei Tykhy† in the Ukraine and of Aleksandr Ginzburg† in Moscow, followed—the day of the CBS interview—by that of Professor

Yuri Orlov,† founder of the Soviet Helsinki Accord monitoring groups. The groups, their activity, and Sakharov's appeals for them are discussed in Chapter X.

One week after the CBS interview—February 17—Dr. Sakharov was invited to the U.S. Embassy in Moscow to receive an answer President Carter wrote him from the White House, February 5:

Dear Professor Sakharov:

I received your letter of January 21, and I want to express my appreciation to you for bringing your thoughts to my personal attention.

Human rights is a central concern of my administration. In my inaugural address I stated: "Because we are free, we can never be indifferent to the fate of freedom elsewhere." You may rest assured that the American people and our government will continue our firm commitment to promote respect for human rights not only in our country but also abroad.

We shall use our good offices to seek the release of prisoners of conscience, and we will continue our efforts to shape a world responsive to human aspirations in which nations of differing cultures and histories can live side by side in peace and justice.

I am always glad to hear from you, and I wish you well.

Sincerely,
Jimmy Carter

Elated, Sakharov released the text of the President's letter to Western journalists in Moscow and that day wrote out his reply to Carter:

Dear Mr. President:

Your letter of February 5, which I received today, is a great honor for me and support for the unified human-rights movement in the USSR and the countries of Eastern Europe, of which we consider ourselves a part. In your letter, as earlier in your inaugural speech and other public statements, you have confirmed the adherence of the new American Administration to the principles of human rights throughout the world. Your efforts to assist in freeing prisoners of conscience are particularly significant.

When you were elected, I wrote in a congratulatory telegram of the profound respect which your position evokes in us. Several times I have written and said that the defense of fundamental human rights is not interference in the internal affairs of other countries, but rather one of the most important international concerns, inseparable from the basic problems of peace and progress. Today, having received your letter—and I fully understand its exceptional nature—I can only repeat this once again.

I shall also use this opportunity to mention specific cases, including those prisoners of conscience about whom I wrote you in January. One of them, Sergei Kovalev, has a dangerous tumor. I ask you to intercede for his immediate transfer to the prison hospital in Leningrad. Once again, I stress the arbitrary selection of names. Actually, I do not believe I have the right to make such a choice. The fate of many, many political prisoners requires equal attention.

Four members of the Helsinki Watch Groups were arrested in February—Aleksandr Ginzburg, Mykola Rudenko, Oleksei Tykhy, and group leader Yuri Orlov. Their arrest is a challenge to all the states signatory to the Helsinki Accord. I ask you to appeal for the release on surety or bail of Ginzburg and Rudenko, both of whom are ill. It is essential that heads of all governments which signed the Helsinki Accord take active measures to obtain the release of all members of the group so that it can continue its important work.

From foreign radio broadcasts, I learned that you expressed the desire to meet me if I should come to the USA. I am very grateful for this invitation. Without doubt, such a visit and personal contacts would have special significance for me. Unfortunately, at the present time, I do not foresee any chance of my taking such a trip.

I want to express the hope that the efforts of people of good will, as well as your personal efforts, Mr. President, will promote the realization of those lofty aims of which you wrote me. With deep respect,

> Sincerely,
> Andrei Sakharov

Dr. Sakharov also added his Moscow address (48B Chkalov Street, Apt. 68) and telephone number (227-27-20) to his signature, and in a February 23 interview with a correspondent of France-Soir, he analyzed the meaning of his correspondence with the President and the limits of his role in advising the West:

Q: What has changed for you personally and for the struggle after the Carter letter?

A: Concretely—nothing. For myself, personally—nothing. For the struggle, I imagine that it is a matter of time. Those moral criteria which, as President Carter stated in his letter, will be the basis of the activities of the new Administration are very important not only for the moment, but in the long term. When the President of a great country speaks of it, interest in human rights can only grow, and that is very good.

But I would like to see actual, rapid solutions to those questions where speed is essential. I wrote in reply to the President to ask him to intercede immediately to effect the transfer of Sergei Kovalev, who is gravely ill. But Kovalev is still in Camp 36 and still on a hunger strike. Only an immediate transfer to a hospital can save his life. In my letter, I also asked for help in freeing Aleksandr Ginzburg and Mykola Rudenko on surety or bail. Seven people—among them my wife and I—have asked the Procuracy about this, but have received no reply. I wrote that the four members of the Helsinki Watch Groups in the USSR should be released so that the group could continue its important work. However, all four are in prison. I am certain that these three specific issues can be resolved without affecting the SALT negotiations and must be dealt with as soon as possible.

Unfortunately, since this has not occurred, I cannot say that anything has changed after the President's letter to me.

Q: What can the West do?

A: It seems to me that I cannot give advice—any more than anyone could living in our country or in Eastern Europe. Western leaders, Western public figures, are simply better informed than we are. They don't live under pressure, under the yoke of repressions, without a free press, without postal or telephone connections. We can't give advice. We speak out—and loudly—about what is going on here, and just to speak the truth here is very difficult in itself. By speaking out, we are defending peace and the future. But as to drawing conclusions about what should be done—that the West must decide for itself.

A month later, March 25, an ABC News correspondent asked if the exchange with Carter had been, as many in the West were saying, counterproductive:

Q: Since Carter became President, some dissidents have been arrested and you have been threatened with criminal prosecution yourself. Some say that President Carter's position on human rights has led the Soviet government to put stronger pressure on the dissidents. Do you agree?

A: Categorically—no! Repressions are our daily life. They existed under Nixon, under Ford, and both before and after Helsinki. The latest wave of repressions began during the first days of January—that is, before Carter took office. Of course, by having made public statements on human rights, Carter did assume a certain responsibility.

But if specific actions do not follow general statements, if the public in America and in Europe—legislatures, business people, scientific and cultural organizations in charge of contacts, and labor unions—do not support these statements and the principles expressed in them, then not only will these people in prison not be freed, but a further intensification of repression may occur.

Q: Many Soviet commentators say that Carter's letter to you is interference in the internal affairs of the USSR. Do you agree?

A: A personal letter—in which the USSR is not even

mentioned—can in no way be interference in its internal affairs.

Dr. Sakharov's estimate of the diplomatic niceties involved in his correspondence with the President was not shared by the Soviet government. The day that the President's letter was released in Moscow, Soviet Ambassador Anatoly Dobrynin called at the State Department to lodge what press accounts called a heated protest. It was followed by others in the Soviet press, including a major commentary in Pravda, the official party organ. In a speech on March 22, Leonid Brezhnev personally denounced "outright attempts by official American agencies to interfere in the internal affairs of the Soviet Union." He said the Soviet Union "will never tolerate interference . . . by any country under any pretext," but especially not under cover of "a clamor being raised about the so-called 'dissidents' and about the 'violation of human rights' in socialist countries."

In Washington the effect of the exchange was both to make the Administration's human-rights policy front-page news and to call the policy's wisdom and execution into public question.

That debate has continued well into the Administration's second year in office, but its outlines were apparent from the first month. Six days after the Inauguration, the State Department issued a statement of concern for the promoters of Charter '77, followed the next day by the "unauthorized" admonition to Moscow that "any attempts . . . to intimidate Mr. Sakharov . . . long admired as an outspoken champion of human rights . . . will conflict with accepted international standards." When the correspondence between the White House and Chkalov Street became public, critics of President Carter were quick to call his policy improvised and to warn against unnecessarily provoking the Kremlin.

Arthur Schlesinger, Jr., wrote in the Wall Street Journal *of March 4 that the President's stance "must be judged thus far . . . a considerable and very serious success. . . . His letter to Sakharov obviously expressed real personal concern. It also registered widespread public sentiment in* the United States and elsewhere. For human rights is evidently one of those ideas whose day has finally arrived." But the historian and one-time White House adviser quickly cautioned that the letter to Sakharov did not seem to be "part of a thought-out policy," that the policy should not "seem just one more stick with which to beat the Russians" and that "official sermons to the world may encourage us in the delusion that we are morally superior to everybody else."

James Reston in his New York Times column of February 19 wrote that the letter to Sakharov "has sent a polite shudder through the entire diplomatic fraternity. The best they can say for [Carter] is that maybe it was an innocent mistake of inexperience." Mr. Reston also reported the statement of National Security adviser Zbigniew Brzezinski that the response to Dr. Sakharov had been "thought through" and was "prudential." Brzezinski viewed the letter as being not as "pointed and provocative" as a public reply, and said it had been necessary to write, since to ignore the Sakharov letter would have been "scarcely reasonable." Admiringly, Reston concluded that even though the exchange "raises some awkward questions," it shows the President's "assumption that if the Soviet Union can be diverted by a letter to Sakharov from trying to get control of the world arms traffic, maybe an arms agreement would not mean all that much."

More critical, Joseph Kraft commented in the Washington Post on February 24 that the President "seems not to have fully assessed . . . the scope [of] the issue of human rights in the Communist world" and was "unprepared for a vigorous response" from the Soviets to his actions and statements. "The human rights factor," Kraft wrote, "is far too important to be handled on a one-shot, tit-for-tat basis without a thorough exploration of effects and side-effects on such issues as arms control. . . . A President is probably better off burnishing the [American] record from time to time on an impersonal basis than being a compulsive talker."

In short, Sakharov's letter—written in haste and not meant for publication—became the catalyst for a major debate on U.S. foreign policy, an argument which still con-

tinues on the role of human-rights advocacy in furthering or impeding East-West relations. In the view of one unnamed State Department official quoted by Robert K. Kaiser in the Washington Post on February 27, 1977: "The whole thing has grown like Topsy and seems to be feeding on itself." In fact, both Sakharov's initiative and Carter's response appear, in retrospect, to have been the natural, almost inevitable convergence of two human-rights campaigners destined to come together.

V

The Subway Bomb

If Washington commentators and Soviet observers were initially confused about the Carter Administration's commitment to human rights, Sakharov and his closest associates were for a time deeply alarmed. The cause of the anxiety was not a State Department declaration of January 27 expressing concern for Sakharov's safety, but the almost immediate appearance of what looked like a high-level recantation of the support.

The episode, the details of which appear in this chapter, began with a bomb explosion in the Moscow subway on January 8 and a seemingly authorized story linking the blast to dissident activity. In response to that insinuation, Sakharov countercharged that the KGB could be intending to use the explosion as a pretext for a new crackdown on dissenters. And for his temerity in advancing such an idea, Sakharov himself was called in by Soviet officials for a formal dressing-down and a warning of possible legal consequences.

At this point, the State Department—simultaneously adopting a new press-relations policy and a new rhetorical vigor on human-rights matters—routinely posted in its press room on January 27 a written answer to a question posed by a correspondent the day before, the day when news of Sakharov's warning in Moscow had been published in Washington. The statement said: "We have long admired Andrei Sakharov as an outspoken champion of human rights in the Soviet Union. He is, as you know, a prominent, respected scientist, a Nobel laureate, who, at considerable risk, has worked to promote respect for human rights in his native *land. Any attempt by the Soviet authorities to intimidate Mr. Sakharov will not silence legitimate criticism in the Soviet Union and will conflict with accepted standards of human rights."*

That same Thursday evening, Soviet Ambassador Dobrynin telephoned Secretary of State Vance to complain about the statement. The next day Vance, who was awaiting word from the Kremlin on his bid to go to Moscow to resume SALT talks, let it be known that he was upset to have been confronted by a protest over a statement he had not even seen after its release, much less cleared in advance. "Inside" stories blossomed in the U.S. press about what one "senior official" characterized to a reporter as "a glitch in our system."

To Sakharov, getting the information in fragments over the Western radio, it seemed that the U.S. government was turning away from him. The impression and tension deepened when newsmen on a helicopter trip with President Carter from Pittsburgh back to Washington, on Sunday, January 30, reported that Carter approved the State Department position as "my attitude," but felt, "Perhaps it should have been said by myself or Secretary Vance." As reported by The New York Times, the President, in an informal exchange, asserted that "we're not going to back down" on the human rights issue, but also disapproved of "publicity stunts meant to goad" or "preaching to governments." Carter was also quoted as saying that it was important for the Soviet Union to understand accurately "our deep commitment to human rights and our inclination to be at peace with the Soviet Union on the other hand."

Within a few days, the incident was more or less forgotten. The Administration clarified its stand in stronger comments by both the Secretary and the President, and on February 5, Carter sent his own letter directly to Sakharov. Until it was received, however, the physicist lived with considerable uncertainty about the effect of the episode he touched off with the following statement, issued January 12, at the height of his concern over the aftershock from the bomb blast in the Moscow subway:

On January 8, an explosion took place in a Moscow subway car. TASS announced that the explosion had been small and that there had been victims who were given medical aid. Nevertheless, it is now evident that the event was, in fact, of more serious proportions. According to oral accounts of eyewitnesses circulating in Moscow, no fewer than four people—and possibly seven or eight—were killed, among them a little boy who was in Moscow for the holidays; dozens of others were seriously injured.

From the various sources there emerges one fairly constant account of the event, essentially the following. Passengers in the car in which the explosion took place noticed two young men (according to another version, three young men and a young woman) get off at Izmailovskaya Station, leaving a briefcase behind on a seat. Several minutes later, the explosion took place. This version rules out accident or carelessness as well as, in my opinion, the possibility that the explosion was either the work of a single madman acting alone or in any way unprofessional.

The TASS announcement of the explosion appeared January 10, two days after the event. Also on the 10th, Victor Louis, well known for his KGB contacts, published an article in the London *Evening News* in which he attributed to unnamed official Soviet sources the contention that Soviet dissidents were responsible for this terrible crime. Unfortunately, this clearly provocative version subsequently was repeated by certain Western information agencies.

I do not know what the KGB plans to do next. I do, however, feel that it has now become essential to call the attention of world public opinion to several important facts which, taken together, leave no doubt as to who, in reality, bears the responsibility for acts of terror, provocation, forgery, intimidation, and slander.

A certain measure of success has marked the struggle for human rights in the USSR and Eastern Europe over the last few years. The Helsinki Accord opened new opportunities in this direction. Now the world knows more about human-rights violations in this part of the globe and understands better than ever that without the worldwide defense of human rights there can be no international trust or security.

The struggle for human rights in Czechoslovakia, the USSR, Poland, and East Germany is based on legal, constitutional precepts. It is both advancing psychological liberation and laying the groundwork for urgently needed democratic reform. It is especially relevant that the activity of those who are commonly called dissidents, who struggle in these countries for human rights, is based on a total, principled rejection of force or the advocacy of violence. Our main goal as well as our only weapon is public discussion, based on accurate information as complete as possible. This consistent and principled position is at the heart of the dissidents' success and moral authority.

Precisely for these reasons, those official agencies dedicated to crushing freedom of thought and fortifying totalitarianism cannot oppose dissidents on legal grounds or through open and honest dialogue. I am convinced that this situation is the cause of lawless closed trials, of groundless sentences, cruel regimens in prisons and labor camps, exile, psychiatric abuse, job dismissals. But the moral authority of dissidents continues to grow in our countries and throughout the world. Under these conditions—as too much evidence proves—government repression has begun to resort more and more to increasingly harsh, purely criminal methods of action. They are reminiscent not only of Italy and Germany under Fascism, but of our own country during those very same years.

The methods are attack, beating, forgery, provocation, defamation, threats of murder, and, apparently, even the commission of political murder. At least five persons have died in suspicious circumstances in the past year: Biblenko,† who belonged to a Baptist congregation persecuted by the authorities; the unemployed jurist Evgeni Brunov, who died only a few hours after he had visited me; the Lithuanian engineer Tamonis,† who had been harassed by the KGB; the teacher and active Lithuanian Catholic Lukshaite†; and the well-known poet-translator Konstantin Bogatyrev,† a former Stalinist camp inmate who exasperated the authorities by his free association and friendship with foreigners. In all these cases, let it be noted, we have heard nothing of inquests or searches for the perpetrators. In my opinion, it is impossible to explain these events as ordinary criminal acts.

The responsibility of the agencies of repression will become even clearer if one remembers how often they resort to murder threats. Merely a few examples: Written on a New Year's greeting card received by Aleksandr Galich's mother: "It has been decided to kill your son." [The writer Lev] Kopelev was victimized by threats when Konstantin Bogatyrev lay on his deathbed. Threats were directed at the pregnant wife of the Georgian dissident [Zviad] Gamsakhurdia.† My family and I have been the targets of countless threats. (Just today we again received a packet of twelve similar letters, this time allegedly from Norway, although this year we received not a single New Year's greeting from Norway or any other country.)

No less repulsive is the slander aimed at discrediting dissidents in the eyes of trusting and uninformed people in the USSR and the West. Recently, the Soviet press, without any foundation, accused Vladimir Bukovsky† of forming a terrorist group. Today I can perceive a link between this accusation and Victor Louis' last article. Aleksandr Ginzburg,† Yuri Orlov,† and the Helsinki Watch Groups have been repeatedly slandered. The deceitful reports that searches conducted at the apartment of Group members produced proof of their ties with the NTS [the émigré People's Labor Alliance—Ed.] were transmitted by TASS even before the searches took place. During the last year, my wife has been the object of unconscionable slander in TASS bulletins, in the Soviet press, in the pro-Soviet press abroad, and in mendacious letters sent to hundreds of addresses allegedly from abroad.

The practice of planting foreign currency, pornography, and the like during searches is a new phenomenon. However, earlier searches bore telltale signs of an underworld mentality. It is impossible to count the number of typewriters and tape recorders confiscated without court order and never returned to their owners. The last search of Aleksandr Ginzburg's apartment set a new record; in addition to the customary typewriter and tape recorder, the police seized five thousand rubles in cash designated to aid the families of political prisoners, and all Ginzburg's personal funds and a radio set as well.

Western readers have become accustomed to the idea that various extremist organizations and gangs of lawbreakers exist in their countries, as do official government agencies which—save for a few tragic exceptions—uphold the law. And it is difficult for these readers to believe and comprehend that here things are completely different—that the handful of people who gather annually on Pushkin Square to demonstrate their respect for the law and the country's constitution are the dissidents, and that those who drive them away are the agents of authority. From this incomprehension stem the confusion and the often uncritical attitude which greet such officially inspired provocations as Victor Louis' article.

I cannot shake off the deep sense that the explosion in the Moscow subway with its tragic deaths is a new provocation of the agencies of repression—the most dangerous in recent years. It is precisely this sensation, and the companion fear that this provocation might lead to a change in the country's domestic climate, that has prompted this article. I would be very happy to have my concern proved false.

In any event, I would like to hope that the criminal acts of the repressive organs neither reflect a new policy bent on crushing dissent for fomenting an "atmosphere of public fury" against them, nor indicate that this policy is one with official sanction from above. Instead, I would like to think that this was just criminal adventurism played out by a certain circle seeking to advance its own power and influence while incapable of engaging in an honest struggle with ideas.

I call on world public opinion to demand an open and public investigation, with the assistance of foreign experts and jurists, of the Moscow explosion of January 8. I hope that world public attention, comprehension of the peculiarities of our system, and the solidarity of all honest people the world over will put a stop to this dangerous development of events. I appeal to people to speak out against crime, provocation, and slander, thus in defense not only of dissidents in the USSR and Eastern Europe, but of the policy of détente, international trust, and the future of mankind.

Although Victor Louis denied that he had suggested in print or otherwise that "dissidents" had any involvement with the explosion, the Soviet dissidents themselves echoed Sakharov's profound anxiety that they were being tarred with responsibility for an act of violence—a tactic they had always denounced—and that the Western press was unthinkingly abetting the smear campaign. As reported in issue No. 44 of The Chronicle of Current Events, *Leonid Borodin, a former political prisoner convicted for membership in a Russian Christian-nationalist organization, issued a statement one day before Sakharov's, accusing Western media of "extreme irresponsibility" in retailing the Louis report. "If someone had decided to do away with all forms of opposition to the USSR," Borodin wrote, "then they would begin precisely with this sort of behavior, terrorist attacks. . . . The West must understand that what strikes it as a bit of sensation is, in this case, a matter of our very existence."*

Two days after the Sakharov statement, spokesmen for the Soviet Helsinki Watch Group and other groups appealed as well for the press to be careful never to confuse nonviolent dissent with terrorism. Jointly, Major General Pyotr Grigorenko† and Professor Yuri Orlov warned that the "situation is dangerously reminiscent of the Reichstag fire." In fact, in the days after the explosion, investigators had conducted what the Chronicle *termed "warrantless interrogations" of three former political prisoners living outside Moscow and of Vladimir Albrecht, the secretary of the capital's branch of Amnesty International. Moreover, Kronid Lyubarsky,† reporting to local police after he was*

*released from Vladimir Prison on January 22, was told that
had he gotten out a bit sooner, he would have had to present an alibi for the day of the explosion.*

*The interrogation that most alarmed the Sakharov
family involved Vladimir Rubtsov, a close friend of Yankelevich's. In a press-conference statement on January 18, Sakharov explained what was happening to Rubtsov:*

In my statement of January 12, I voiced my alarm that
the KGB might use the January 8 subway explosion as a
pretext to step up pressure against dissidents.

Today I can say that my fears have begun to be borne
out.

I would like to introduce you to Vladimir Rubtsov, a
close friend of my son-in-law, Efrem Yankelevich, and a
good friend of my family. Rubtsov is a worker, an elec-
trician, married, with a year-old son; he is thirty-eight. Four
days after the explosion in the Moscow subway, that is, two
days after the TASS statement and the Victor Louis article,
two KGB men came to his apartment and asked where he
had been on Saturday, the day of the explosion. They also
added that he should try to remember exactly, since it was
important. Still, they refused to explain why they were
interested. They only said that it was important in connection with some incident involving public transport.

Rubtsov answered that he had been at home, to which
they replied, "Your brother doesn't confirm that."

Later, it was ascertained that Rubtsov's brother had
refused as an ethical matter to answer questions unrelated
to him and had not denied in any way that his brother had
been home. The men returned with the same questions on
January 16, when Rubtsov's brother told them that Vladimir
Rubtsov had spent all of January 8 at home. These conversations with Rubtsov and his brother were marked by thinly
disguised threats and were full of allusions to Rubtsov's involvement in certain unspecified events.

A month and a half earlier, on November 30, 1976, a search was conducted in the building where Rubtsov's brother lives, in the village of Kupavna in the Moscow oblast (Rubtsov himself is only registered there; he lives most of the time at his wife's apartment in Moscow). Rubtsov was not there at the time. His brother was told that the search was connected with the theft of some weapons from a local school. No weapons were found, yet the searchers demanded that the brother show them Rubtsov's room, and despite his refusal, the room was searched.

A series of manuscripts and *samizdat* texts were seized, including several statements and interviews by me which I had given Rubtsov at various times. After the search, Rubtsov's brother and his wife, and Rubtsov and his wife, Tatiana Postnikova, were all summoned for interrogation on several occasions. Rubtsov was questioned mostly about the seized materials: who had given them to him and to whom he had given them to read. The others were questioned about Rubtsov's acquaintances. Rubtsov's wife was told that her husband had embarked on the path of crime and that no Yankelevich could help him. Later they stated that they knew Rubtsov and Yankelevich had intentions of making a public protest, but that it would not help anyone and would only bring Rubtsov trouble. Efrem Yankelevich had in fact written and sent an open letter to public human-rights organizations and the AFL-CIO in which he appealed for the defense of Vladimir Rubtsov and the principle of the free exchange of information.

This is a short statement of facts on the illegal persecution of Rubtsov.

I fear for Rubtsov's fate, as for someone who is a friend of Efrem Yankelevich and a frequent guest of our family. Unfortunately, the fate of other friends of ours has shown that there are grounds for my apprehension. I am especially alarmed that the incident of January 8 is being used as a form of pressure on Rubtsov.

P.S. After we had already invited you yesterday to come, we learned that Rubtsov had been summoned to appear today at the Moscow Municipal Procurator's Office for interrogation.

Yankelevich's letter of December 27, 1976, was addressed to the International League for Human Rights, Amnesty International, the German Society to Defend Human Rights, and the AFL-CIO. In it he wrote of the November search and subsequent interrogations of Rubtsov and of his own and Rubtsov's right to exchange information freely. Excerpts follow:

". . . I cannot view the threats worded in the course of these 'talks' (by the KGB with Rubtsov) as simply an everyday, and moreover illegal, investigative tactic. Most of the well-known political trials in recent years and in 1976—Dzhemilev (Omsk), Tverdokhlebov (Moscow), Igrunov (Odessa), Bashkirov (Yakutsk)—have shown that the authorities view the possession of any scrap of paper containing the expression of a single idea contradicting any official doctrine in the arts, ideology, politics, or economics as a state crime which warrants cruel punishment. Dzhemilev, for example, was punished for possessing a draft manuscript written in Arabic script with the intent to disseminate it.

"Thus, the public statements of Nobel Laureate Andrei Sakharov (articles, announcements, interviews), the writings of Solzhenitsyn, of [Evgeni] Zamiatin, an Orwell story, and an issue of The Chronicle of Current Events seized during the search of Vladimir Rubtsov's apartment are all evidence for a criminal case which has either already been initiated or which can be set in motion whenever the authorities choose. . . .

"In speaking out in defense of Vladimir Rubtsov and, thereby, relying on your support, I am also defending my right to the free exchange of information. I feel that this right has been violated regardless of whether V. Rubtsov and I ever conducted such an exchange. . . . I risk an even more general assertion: the violation of one person's right to exchange information freely constitutes an infringement on everyone's right to do so. . . .

"Therefore, I have considered and still consider it my right to read and disseminate any materials, whether in manuscript or printed form, regardless of government approval or disapproval. Since access to uncensored publica-

tions is obstructed for the majority of my fellow citizens, I consider it my duty to disseminate these as well. . . .

" 'The state has the right to defend itself' is a slogan that the authorities have recently used to justify their punitive policies in the area of informational exchange. I cannot take this statement seriously. I do not know of a single political trial at which the defendant was charged with disseminating an appeal for the violent overthrow of the existing system, for war, or for class or racial hatred. . . .

"Nevertheless, by asserting its specific right, the state tries to give the soothing impression that it is wisely limiting its own boundless power by recognizing some form of civil rights. This has not occurred in fact. Nor will it, as long as the authorities continue to view each uncensored work as an assault on their ideology or prestige, or on the nation's domestic political unity, and as long as they fail to repudiate force in their struggle. . . ."

On February 16, 1977, Yankelevich was interrogated in connection with the "Rubtsov case." Following is his account, written the next day, of that interrogation:

"Around 3:00 in the afternoon, I was summoned to the Municipal Procuracy by Investigator Ponomarev and interrogated as a witness in the case on 'materials seized during the search of Citizen Rubtsov's apartment which are presumed to be slanderous in nature, and on all circumstances relating to him.' (This is the approximate wording of the protocol.)

"Below is an account of the interrogation, with the investigator's questions as entered in the protocol (as I remember them) and my answers (recorded exactly), with some additional commentary.

"Question: *Are you acquainted with Citizen Rubtsov?*

"Answer: *I refuse to give evidence on the grounds that I cannot take part in a case aimed at infringing on the right to exchange information.* (In explaining my stance and in responding to Ponomarev's questions, I referred to the unlawful nature of existing judicial practice with relation to

Article 190.1, specifically to the cases of Amalrik, Dzhemilev, and Bashkirov; also, I explained that Article 190.1, as it stands, contradicts the RSFSR Constitution and the International Covenant. The investigator's arguments, as I understood them, all were based on the fact that the Supreme Soviet of the USSR or the RSFSR had legally adopted and confirmed the article.)

"Question: *Did you give Rubtsov any of the materials seized at his apartment—materials whose dissemination on Soviet territory is prohibited?*

"Answer: *I refuse to answer that question for the reasons I just gave you.*

"This was my response to each of the following questions.

"Question: (*Something about Rubtsov or the seized materials*).

"Question: *What do you know about 'Khronika Press'?*

"Question: *Are you familiar with issue no. 22 of* The Chronicle of Human Rights in the USSR?

"Question: *Do you admit to the authorship of a statement which bears your signature* (*Ponomarev handed me a copy of issue no. 22 of* The Chronicle *which had printed my statement on the attempt to fabricate a criminal case— never pursued after my statement was publicized—against me for allegedly causing an automobile accident*) *published in issue no. 22?*

"Question: *Did you transmit this statement abroad?*

"Question: *Who transmitted it, and what was your purpose in featuring this statement in this publication?*

"Question: *Are you familiar with the criminal cases of Feldman, Timchuk, Shtern,† Roitburd, and Dzhvarsheishvili, and on what grounds do you slanderously allege that the KGB engages in 'the practice of fabricating criminal cases to retaliate against and compromise individuals who bother them?'* (*When I expressed my bewilderment at the question, Investigator Ponomarev explained that he was not accusing me of slander, but that he had to phrase his question this way because, in refusing to give evidence, I had not cited any proof of the innocence of those whom the court had found guilty of criminal conduct.*)

"When I learned that the interrogation was complete, I said that I wanted to make several additions to the protocol . . . to indicate that many of his questions had no relation to the case described at the beginning of the interrogation. Investigator Ponomarev said that I was mistaken, and that had I only answered his questions, he would have asked me others which would have shown me the connection between Rubtsov's search and my statement in The Chronicle of Human Rights. *He then wrote down another question: Did you acquaint Citizen Rubtsov with the statement referred to here? (Neither issue no. 22 of* The Chronicle of Human Rights *nor my statement figured in the search record on the list of materials confiscated. In my opinion, Ponomarev's last question also failed to establish any link between my statement and the materials of the search. The search, incidentally, was conducted with 'the aim of seizing firearms' allegedly in the possession of Vladimir Rubtsov's brother, Aleksandr.)*

"I wrote: 'Having been warned of my liability for refusing to give evidence, I would like to note that most of the questions asked, specifically from the fourth one on, in my opinion had no relation to the case. . . .' This was the final notation in the protocol of the interrogation, which lasted approximately two hours."

A week after the Rubtsov press conference, Sakharov again called Western journalists to his apartment to receive a statement on the "formal and critically serious warning" he had been given that day to stop suggesting any tie between the KGB and the subway blast:

On January 24, I was served with a notice to appear at the Procuracy of the USSR on January 25 at 3:00 p.m. I was escorted to the offices of the Deputy Procurator General of the USSR, G. I. Gusev. Another man was present; in the course of the conversation, Gusev identified him as chief of the Procuracy's Investigation Section.

Following is an account, reconstructed from memory, the same day:

Gusev announced: "We have not called you in to extract explanations. We have long known about your activities, and I particularly stress the word *activities*. The purpose of the summons is to give you an official warning.

"Recently, you issued and widely disseminated a statement which is being used by hostile foreign propaganda. In this statement you monstrously and slanderously alleged that the explosion in the Moscow subway was a provocation, the work of official agencies, in particular," he added with acute embarrassment, "the organs of state security, supposedly acting on instructions from above." (I tried to get him to be more specific,* but Gusev said that he had to finish with the warning.) "You slanderously maintained that the explosion was a provocation directed against the so-called dissidents with the aim of changing the domestic climate of the country. You are required to disavow your deliberately false statement by publishing a correction in any manner you can.

"This was not your first hostile, slanderous, and criminal act. Some time ago you were warned by the Deputy Procurator General of the USSR, Comrade Malyarov. But you have continued to carry out acts which are punishable as crimes under Soviet law.

"You are abusing our patience. Today I am presenting you with your second formal and critically serious warning. You must draw the logical conclusions. Otherwise, you will be held legally responsible. Look it over and sign." Gusev then placed before me a piece of paper with approximately the following text:

WARNING

Citizen A. D. Sakharov is hereby warned that he has issued a deliberately false statement in which he alleged that the explosion in the Moscow subway was a provocation devised by government agencies directed against so-called dissidents. Citizen A. D. Sakharov is warned that the continuation and repetition

* That is, to name the Committee on State Security (KGB).—Ed.

of his criminal acts will result in his liability in accordance with the law of the land.

> 1. Counselor of Justice First Class,
>   Deputy Procurator General of
>   the USSR S. I. Gusev (signature).
>
> 2. ....
>   (line for my signature).

The document was not dated.

After reading the document, I said the following:

"I refuse to sign this document. First of all, I must clarify your description of my last statement. In it, I did not directly accuse the KGB of being responsible for planning the explosion in the Moscow subway, but I did express a certain apprehension (or 'deep sense' as I wrote). But I also expressed hope that the event was not sanctioned from above.

"I am conscious of the critical nature of my statement, which I do not regret having written. Critical situations demand critical means. If my statement results in an objective investigation ending with the true perpetrators found and the innocent spared—if a provocation against dissidents does not materialize—I will be very grateful. I now have serious reasons for apprehension: Victor Louis' provocation-like article in the London *Evening News*, which has not yet been retracted by the paper; the recent interrogations of individuals I am certain were not involved about their whereabouts at the time of the blast; the numerous murders over the past few months in which KGB involvement seems conceivable, murders which have not been investigated. I will mention two of them: the murders of poet Konstantin Bogatyrev and jurist Evgeni Brunov. You have said nothing of these murders, which are central to my reasoning.

"I remind you that the KGB bears officially acknowledged responsibility for countless thousands of very grave crimes in the recent past. I am sure that the situation justified my statement, that it was crucial at the time. I would like to copy the warning for my records. The document is not marked classified."

Gusev: This warning is designated only for you. It should not be copied.

Sakharov: You evidently feel that the document compromises the Procuracy.

Gusev: I did not say that. (Reaching out:) Sign, please.

Sakharov: I refuse to sign.

Gusev: That is your affair. You have been issued a second serious warning and you must draw the proper conclusions. Treat the warning with utmost seriousness. I have signed the document and it will remain in the Procuracy's files.

Markov: You do know that dissemination of deliberately false inventions is punishable by law. In this country no one is tried for nothing.

Sakharov: My experience shows otherwise. With whom am I speaking?

Gusev: This is Markov, the chief of the Procuracy's Investigation Section. You have already received one warning inside these walls, but you have failed to heed it.

Sakharov: Malyarov mostly spoke about my staying away from foreigners. I said then that there was nothing to take seriously.

Gusev: Why do you refuse to sign the warning?

Sakharov: It is impossible for me to sign a text which describes my activity as criminal. I never do anything that violates the law. My activity has received worldwide recognition. I have been honored with the Nobel Peace Prize. I will continue my activity in accordance with the dictates of my conscience.

Gusev: You may be mistaken.

Sakharov: I am sure that you are the one who is mistaken. Goodbye.

Gusev: Goodbye.

The meeting at the Procuracy lasted twenty-five minutes.

The day after the interview the Soviet press opened a print assault on Sakharov, reminiscent of the public cam-

paign against him at the time of his first official warning in August 1973. The following brief announcement appeared in several Soviet newspapers on that date in both Izvestia, the official, nationally circulated government paper, and in the popular afternoon paper published by the Moscow city authorities, Vechernaya Moskva, on January 26:

A SLANDERER IS WARNED

A. D. Sakharov was summoned to the Procuracy of the USSR on January 25. S. I. Gusev, Deputy Procurator General of the USSR and State Counselor of Justice First Class, warned him that the provocation he has made in statement form contains *deliberately false slanderous inventions which discredit the Soviet state and social system*. [*Emphasis added to the verbatim wording of Article 190.1 of the RSFSR Criminal Code.—Ed.*] Sakharov has been apprised of the inadmissibility of such slanderous activity in the future. If he ignores the warning issued him, he will be held criminally responsible before Soviet law.

On January 20, the international service of TASS carried an article ("About a Certain Anti-Soviet Uproar") by commentator Yuri Kornilov, who had been an active contributor in the 1973 campaign. The article, typical of official, public Soviet reaction to Western criticism of human-rights matters in the USSR, links Sakharov's conduct to the anti-Soviet machinations of dedicated Western Cold Warriors. The full text follows:

This is not the first time we have encountered the attempts of certain groups, for the most part Zionist or other reactionary organizations, to promote the idea that the Soviet Union has set out to violate the [Helsinki Conference] Final Act [of August 1, 1975] virtually since the moment it signed the document. As if to confirm this thoroughly fallacious thesis, these groups raise the issue of human rights in the USSR, the "defense" of those the West calls dissidents who allegedly appeal within the Soviet Union for the consistent realization of the Helsinki principles.

The slogan of the "defense of the Helsinki agreements in the USSR" is nothing more than a decoy. In fact, what we have here is an anti-Soviet campaign orchestrated on. U.S. territory by the unified action of certain agencies directly responsible for organizing subversive, ideological, and other types of activities in the Soviet Union and Eastern Europe. This, in fact, is the source of the anti-Soviet furor surrounding the topic of human rights in the USSR. And no matter what the mask, the goal pursued is one and the same: to discredit the Soviet socialist order, the Soviet way of life.

In this campaign, a clear role has been delegated to a small bunch of people living on Soviet territory whose convictions diverge from those held by the vast majority of Soviet people. These individuals, for one reason or another, do not like the Soviet system, and the Soviet way of doing things does not suit them; essentially, they have long been internal émigrés. They are used by special services in the West to inflate the soap bubble of human-rights "violations" occurring in the USSR.

Until the present time, designated individuals have been supported by correspondents of various Western newspapers which, for reasons known only to them, inflame the dissident theme. Clearly, such pronouncements, which constitute flagrant interference into the internal affairs of the Soviet Union, cannot be termed "friendly"; it is unimaginable that any unbiased individual could view this performance as conforming to the agreements reached at Helsinki. But such are the ways of the bourgeois press which represents the interests of separate political groups and bourgeois monopolies.

Astonishingly enough, a representative of the State Department of the U.S.A., who theoretically should reflect the Administration's official viewpoint, just recently joined this unworthy game. With or without the knowledge of its new head, a statement was issued backing the renegade Sakharov and alleging—along with similar delirium—that Sakharov is being threatened with some kind of punishment.

Today the U.S. press reports that the State Department leadership supposedly was not consulted about the statement. Nevertheless, a fact remains a fact: the State Department went and released the statement. An official statement, even! As if to say, "Well, let them figure out whether the statement is true or not." And, according to standard practice, the American mass media managed to trumpet the statement around the world before the ink was even dry.

But what really happened? Let us look at facts. As we have already said, the issue is linked to Sakharov. This gentleman is well known in the West. He is also known in the Soviet Union, where we see all sides of him clearly. One day he composes pasquinades in which he flings dirt at the Soviet people and Soviet state; the next he supplies traveling emissaries with hostile anti-Soviet materials; or on another he is brawling in a fight in the literal sense of the word, as he did not long ago in Siberia.* This time Sakharov attracted attention by announcing that the Soviet authorities, the KGB in particular, allegedly were a party to the recent explosion in the Moscow subway. After this announcement, Sakharov was summoned to the Procuracy of the USSR. There he was warned that his statement was a blatant lie which discredited the Soviet social and state order; that he was deluding worldwide public opinion with his statement; that such activities as his were socially dangerous and criminally punishable under Soviet law.

Characteristically, a series of Western newspapers also noted that Sakharov's slanderous statement provided grounds for bringing charges against him. It was noted in the Western press as well that the dissemination of deliberately false inventions about a government and its agencies is liable to legal punishment in many countries.

Sakharov had positively no foundation for claiming that the organs of state security had been a party to the explosion in the subway—something he actually admitted during his conversation at the Procuracy of the USSR.

A verbatim record of this conversation exists. I will be precise. Here is the relevant part of the record:

Procurator Gusev: Andrei Dmitrivich, I have invited you here officially to warn you about your recent public statement which was disseminated in the foreign press of a number of bourgeois countries. In this statement it is indicated that Soviet authorities, the state security organs in particular, organized the explosion in the Moscow subway as a provocation. . . .

Sakharov: I did not speak of the participation of the organs in the subway explosion. I stated that I have the impression that they were involved. . . . I expressed my opinion not in the form

---

* An allusion to an incident at Omsk. See p. 88.—Ed.

of a statement of fact, but as conjecture. I did not state that it had been sanctioned from above. . . .

As we see, Sakharov hedges and tries to sidestep, confirming in essence that he does not have, nor has ever had, any facts to back up this sort of concoction. The question arises: how did it happen that these filthy inventions were so eagerly snapped up in the West, even by official personages? As we can see, certain Washingtonians are suffering a serious case of anti-Soviet itch and, under the guise of false concern over the implementation of the Helsinki resolutions, work only to slander the USSR and the Soviet way of life.

This, it seems to me, is the essence of the anti-Soviet racket raised in the West, which, by the way, is being played both on the right and on the left by professional anti-Soviet types from bourgeois organs of the press and by those of the leftist ilk. The latter's actions involuntarily force us to recall the words of the well-known Russian artist that there is only one step from leftist extremism to bare-faced rascality.

What can be said in conclusion? The gentlemen who so diligently occupy themselves in the West with the observance of the Helsinki agreement in the USSR should take a 180-degree turn and take a look at how this agreement is being implemented in their own countries, in those countries where millions of unemployed have to eke out a miserable existence and are left without a crumb; where the segregation of blacks and unbridled racism bloom; where synagogues are desecrated, political activists are murdered, millions of files are kept on dissenters. . . . And to those who seize on the inventions of renegades and anti-Soviets to try to slander the USSR, I would like to cite a well-known Russian proverb: Look before you leap, gentlemen!

Sakharov, however, was not without defenders in the Soviet Union—especially among those he had himself sought to defend. On January 28—two days after the Izvestia *announcement—nineteen political prisoners in Vladimir Prison sent their own individual letters of appeal and protest to the Procurator and jointly issued an open letter attacking the threats against the man they called a "well-known political figure." Arguing that his aim was to promote an end to un-*

just persecution and a beginning of democratic order in the USSR, the nineteen inmates wrote in part:

We see the latest threats against Academician Sakharov not just as evidence of the Soviet government's persistent refusal to move toward democratization, but also as a conscious effort to complicate the normalization of international relations, to jeopardize détente as a whole. We stress: the new wave of threats against the opposition—and the threats against Sakharov demonstrate the escalation of the campaign—began in the year of the Belgrade meeting. . . .

In another letter to Deputy Procurator General Gusev, a former political prisoner, Evgeni Borisovich Nikolayev of 5 Bulatnikov Street, Apt. 327, Moscow 113403, wrote on January 29 that Sakharov's defense of others had earned him the support of all. The letter:

I feel it my duty to protest your threats against Andrei Dmitrivich Sakharov, Nobel Peace Prize winner, three-time Hero of Socialist Labor, full member of the Academy of Sciences of the USSR, and distinguished activist in the struggle for human rights in the USSR.

I am among those who have been illegally persecuted in our country. In 1970, I was dismissed from my job without the sanction of the Procurator and deprived of my freedom for refusing to take on "socialist obligations" in honor of the XXIV Congress of the CPSU.

From personal experience and from the experience of many others illegally persecuted, I know that gross violations of human rights are occurring in our country. Therefore the activity of Andrei Dmitrivich Sakharov, in promoting the rule of law, the UN Universal Declaration of Human Rights, the International Covenants on Civil and Political Rights, and the Helsinki Accord, is a critical necessity for our country, essential for those already persecuted for their convictions as well as for those upon whom repressions have not yet fallen, but still may fall.

This is precisely why I consider it vital that I speak up for Andrei Dmitrivich Sakharov. It so happened that Sakharov defended me more than once, although he himself was unaware of those reprisals which befell me personally. When he publicly called for the release of *all* prisoners of conscience in the USSR, he thereby stood up in my behalf as well.

And if *one man* stands up for *every man,* then it is the duty of *every man* to stand up in defense of the *one* when danger threatens *him.*

I appeal to you, Citizen Gusev, to retract your threats against Sakharov.

Almost a month later the Soviet authorities reopened the polemic with an article signed by Deputy Procurator General Gusev, printed on February 23 on the Op-Ed page of The New York Times *under the heading "Moscow, on Sakharov":*

MOSCOW—Immediately after the unprecedented explosion in the Moscow Metro on Jan. 8, Andrei D. Sakharov, without any grounds whatsoever, publicly accused the authorities of being a party to the crime, which, he claimed, was perpetrated to sanction later repression of the "dissidents."

Those statements could not pass unnoticed by the Procurator's Office of the Union of Soviet Socialist Republics, for under the Constitution it exercises supreme supervision over the observance of the laws.

I invited Sakharov to the Procurator's Office on Jan. 25 and explained to him that his provocative statement contained absolutely false and slanderous fabrications subject to Articles 70 and 190 of the penal code of the Russian Federation. The latter, in particular, stipulates responsibility for the systematic spreading of slanderous fabrications derogatory to the Soviet political and social system.

Sakharov was warned in written form that he might be called to account if he ignored this warning and performed acts of a similar nature.

It was not the first time that Sakharov had been invited for such a conversation. Way back on Aug. 16, 1973, he was told in the Procurator's Office of the USSR about the unlawfulness of a whole number of aspects of his activities that took the form of systematic oral and written instigatory and slanderous propaganda with the aim of discrediting the Soviet political system, the peace foreign policy of the Communist Party and the Soviet state, Soviet-United States rapprochement and détente.

I will recall that Sakharov gave all sorts of "advice" to Western political leaders, parliamentarians and United States Congressmen on how they should treat the Soviet Union, often directly calling for political blackmail against the country whose citizen he is.

Thus, the two conversations with Sakharov dealt not with his convictions but with the specific actions contradicting or directly violating Soviet legislation.

Naturally, no sovereign state can look indifferently on such deeds by its citizens. Those who are now assiduously playing up the "Sakharov affair" would do well to recall the legislation of their own countries.

Let us take, for example, the United States Code. Paragraph 2385 of Title 18 reads:

"Whoever knowingly or willfully advocates, abets, advises or teaches the duty, necessity, desirability or propriety of overthrowing or destroying the government of the United States or the government of any state . . . or . . . with intent to cause the overthrow or destruction of any such government, prints, publishes, edits, issues, circulates, sells, distributes, or publicly displays any written or printed matter, advocating, advising or teaching the duty, necessity, desirability, or propriety of overthrowing or destroying any government in the United States by force or violence, or attempts to do so . . . shall be fined not more than $20,000 or imprisoned not more than 20 years or both. . . ."

It is not precluded that were Sakharov a citizen of the United States he might well find himself behind bars.

Similar articles in various interpretations are contained in practically all penal codes of the Western countries. Yet, proceeding from humane considerations, we are so far applying only measures of a moral and preventive nature to Sakharov and some other persons. This fact is often assessed by the foreign press and some "dissidents," including Sakharov, as a result of outside "pressure" on the Soviet authorities, who are supposedly compelled to "reckon with Western public opinion." These are groundless illusions.

Sakharov, in the conversation with me, tried to emphasize his exclusive status and past services, which, he claimed, gave him the right to violate the laws existing in this country. But the principle of citizens' equality before the law in the USSR applies to all without any exception. In that connection, Sakharov was told that he, like any citizen, had not only rights but also duties.

Sakharov's appeal to public opinion in the West, and support of him by the foreign mass information media and even official government offices, are an attempt to put Sakharov into an exceptional position. If Sakharov and his Western defenders think that the Soviet Union will renounce one of the fundamental principles of its juridical system—the equality of all citizens before the law—they are deeply mistaken.

On March 5, the Times *gave space to Valery Chalidze— a physicist now in exile, co-founder with Sakharov of the Moscow Human Rights Committee—to reply to the Gusev article. Chalidze's piece, written in New York where he edits Khronika Press and its* Chronicle of Human Rights in the USSR, *appeared under the headline "What Is This Slander?" In it, Chalidze said that Sakharov was right to question the origins of the subway-bomb incident: "Soviet history contains too many sad precedents. The secret police have organized 'accidents' and murders and provocations."*

Although, in the aftermath of the bomb blast, a number of Soviet human-rights activists were jailed, the most prominent were members of the Helsinki Watch (see Chapter X), arrested or harassed for their efforts in those groups. None has been accused of having any connection to the explosion. In fact, it was not until June 7, 1978, that the Soviet authorities—in a very brief TASS story—disclosed that "several" individuals had been arrested in connection with the explosion and other crimes, had reportedly confessed their involvement, and faced continuing investigation and eventual trial. No other details were given.

VI

Close to Home

The last public round in the Sakharov-Gusev encounter occurred when The New York Times *of March 29, 1977, printed Sakharov's own reply to the Deputy Procurator General, a piece written in Moscow on March 5. Under the headline "Andrei D. Sakharov, on 'This Frightful Situation,'" the article revealed the pressures being brought on the physicist directly and, through harassment of his family, indirectly. This chapter presents documents related to that campaign to penalize Sakharov's outspokenness in the most petty and intimate ways.*

The constant strain begins to show in the reply to Gusev:

In his article published in *The New York Times*, Sergei Gusev elaborated the official position of the Soviet Union's repressive organs towards me personally and, indirectly, towards other dissidents. He particularly sought to stress that this position is immune to interference from "Western protectors."

The Gusev article was written shortly after the publication of President Carter's letter to me and was obviously a reaction to that letter. I am confident that no one in the West, including President Carter, will allow himself to be diverted from the active, global defense of human rights—a chosen path of principle on a matter of decisive importance for the future of mankind. The Gusev letter was an obvious attempt to test the firmness of this position in the West.

The reason I was summoned to the office of the Procurator General of the Soviet Union was my appeal to world public opinion in connection with the Moscow subway explosion and other unsolved crimes. Gusev tendentiously expounds on my statement, but says nothing about my line of argument. His article, written a month and a half after the explosion, gives no information as to whether this crime is under investigation or not. Gusev also passes over in silence the question of whether or not the five murder cases that I mentioned in my statement are being investigated.

During my discussions in the procurator's office, I said I would be profoundly satisfied if my appeal were to lead to a thorough and objective investigation from which no innocent persons suffered. I can only affirm this statement once again. I was aware, of course, that my speaking out in this way would lead to grave consequences for me and my family, but I felt that I had no right to keep silent.

Gusev quotes from the article of the U.S. Code under which I could allegedly be charged if I were an American citizen. That article refers, however, to advocating the violent overthrow of the government, which is something I have never done. Gusev does not quote Articles 70 and 190.1 of the Criminal Code of the RSFSR, under which a great many people have suffered and died in prison for nonviolent activities: for distributing or merely possessing truthful information—books and *samizdat* material; for religious activities; and for desiring to leave the country.

I am prepared to be tried for my overt public activities, although I consider them legal and not subject to the Criminal Code. And I have no illusions about the impartiality of Soviet justice.

But the authorities turn instead, not to an open trial, but to foul and cowardly methods of harassment. Now they have pulled out all the stops: countless anonymous threats of physical reprisal, slanderous press articles and TASS statements, illegal refusal to allow an exchange of living accommodations, criminal proceedings brought against my daughter, and a threat to institute proceedings against her husband.

It is essential that we exchange our two two-room apartments for one four-room apartment of equal space—because we cannot continue to live separately under constant threats of murder against all seven members of the family, including two small children. But precisely because of this, the state agencies will not permit us this completely legal, everyday exchange.

The KGB's involvement in this affair is clearly visible in the coordinated publication of a totally false article by a TASS correspondent. According to the article, we have 30 square meters of housing space per person when in fact we have only 9 square meters per person; the word "exchange" was not even mentioned.

In February, immediately after Gusev's "warning," my daughter Tanya Semyonova was threatened with criminal prosecution, instituted by the Procurator General ostensibly on the basis of an anonymous letter. At the same time, my son-in-law, Efrem Yankelevich, was also threatened with criminal prosecution for distributing "anti-Soviet" materials and for "parasitism." Thus do the authorities, contrary to Gusev's hypocritical statements about the equality of all citizens in the eyes of the law, carry out reprisal measures against the members of my family as a brutal means of revenge and pressure on me.

Despite this frightful situation, which is incomparably more tragic than being held personally responsible for my own actions, I consider it my duty to continue my public activity. I see no other alternative. But I hope that those people in the West who have taken upon themselves the burden of responsibility for defending human rights understand the tragically critical nature of the position of all those, including myself personally, who defend human rights in the USSR and in other countries of Eastern Europe. I also rest my hopes in the leaders of the USSR and other socialist countries, in their sense of responsibility and desire for stability in the world.

Every day now brings new problems. On March 4, *Izvestia* printed a vile and provocative article accusing Jews who sought to emigrate of spying. This is a modern-day version of the Dreyfus Affair. I call upon the world public and upon the heads of state who signed the Helsinki agreement to speak out against this provocation.

I call upon the world to speak out in defense of the arrested members of the Public Group to Promote Observance of the Helsinki Agreement—Ginzburg,† Orlov,† Rudenko,† and Tykhy.†° I call for the defense of Pyotr Ruban and all those prisoners—the Yugoslav writer Mikhailov, the arrested members of Charter '77, and other political prisoners in Eastern Europe and the Soviet Union—about whom I wrote in my letter to the President of the United States.

At the center of my public activities remains my demand for worldwide political amnesty—for freedom for all prisoners of conscience. I consider this a precondition for peace.

Although Sakharov has a son and two daughters from his first marriage, he regularly refers to Elena Bonner's children as his own. They are Tatiana Semyonova Yankelevich (who, with her husband, Efrem, and their two small children, lived with the Sakharovs) and Aleksei (Alyosha) Semyonov, who lived with his own wife and child in Moscow. The Yankelevich family left the USSR to live in the United States in September 1977, and Aleksei Semyonov followed them in March 1978.

Sakharov began to talk to Western reporters in Moscow about the domestic pressures on him several months before his Times article. In an interview December 6, 1976, with Associated Press correspondent George Krimsky (expelled by Soviet authorities two months later), he detailed some of the personal abuse that the Nobel Prize had not spared him:

Krimsky: A year ago you were awarded the Nobel Prize. Two questions. What influence did that have on your struggle in the democratic movement? What influence did it have on your personal struggle in that movement?

Sakharov: The situation is full of contradictions and

° See Chapter X.

contrasts. The long-term effect, the effect on world public opinion, is, in my view, extremely important, profound, and positive. My friends and I are grateful to the Nobel Committee for this lofty award; we are grateful for this support of the principles of our democratic movement. A year ago, on December 10, during the Nobel ceremony, the attention of the whole world was riveted on Oslo, where my wife was appearing, and on Vilnius, where, on that same day, I was standing outside the courtroom doors of Kovalev's trial. This attention was fixed both on our movement and on our difficulties.

At the same time, the authorities have acted as though there had been no change in my public position; in fact, the pressures on me increased. As in the past, I have been denied entrance to trials—of Dzhemilev and of Tverdokhlebov. As in the past, my phone and my mail have been cut off.

Krimsky: When was that?

Sakharov: All this year.

Krimsky: When did it begin?

Sakharov: Communication was first cut in 1974. My telephone links were partially restored during my wife's trip abroad and immediately after the incident in Omsk when, obviously, there was fear of major international protests. But for more than two years now, I have not had a chance—except during short breaks—to speak to anyone abroad. Every conversation is cut off by an eavesdropping KGB operator. And these actions do not just concern me personally; they are a major blow to my public activity, for which a working connection with the West is extraordinarily important. They are, I believe, of public significance; they are a violation of international agreements on telephone communications; and I hope that public protests and the protests of the Postal Union will finally end these violations.

I would like to add that the attitude of the authorities reached its logical culmination yesterday during the traditional demonstration at Pushkin Square. We came to honor with our silence the memory of those killed during the Stalinist terror and to express our solidarity with political prisoners. But this time the authorities staged a provocation. Hundreds of specially trained thugs surrounded and pushed us. Some of us were beaten, some had their glasses broken. They poured snow and mud out of special paper bags on my bare head. Such a thing could not happen without permission from the authorities. I consider it an action sanctioned by the authorities and therefore believe it should be a subject for public attention.

Krimsky: Why did they choose this moment to stage such a provocation? What are your views and theory?

Sakharov: I think they believed for a long time that they could keep the attitudes developing among a large number of people under control by using the quietest possible means. But now they see that the civic influence of the human-rights movement is growing; it is even growing in our country, and the international support it has received is spreading. Even the Communist parties of Italy and France have called for the release of our political prisoners.

It is conceivable that the authorities have now decided to use harsher methods against us.

Krimsky: How did your life change after you received the Nobel Prize?

Sakharov: If you mean my personal life, nothing has changed. I have spoken of how the authorities' attitude changed towards my public appearances—it hasn't changed at all. The same is true of my private life.

To start with, this year I was kept without a residence permit for ten and a half months. True, they have now finally granted me a permit, but I see it as something they were bound to do. I am still wary about where it will ultimately lead.

The pressure on my family has unquestionably continued. New forms of harassment have been articles in the press not only against me, but also against my wife. There have been articles in TASS. For example, one of them was called "Mrs. Bonner's Anti-Soviet Performance." Another article—unfounded and extremely unpleasant in tone—appeared in the émigré newspaper *Russky Golos,* which is published in the United States.

My son-in-law is still jobless. That, indeed, is a form of pressure on our close and intimate family.

There has been no progress on granting me an apartment. I have no home now and have to live in my mother-in-law's apartment. The Academy of Sciences maintains that I cannot be given quarters of any kind because the Moscow City Council objects. At least, that is the pretext cited by the Academy of Sciences, which regularly resolves such questions very simply, without any fuss.

Such is my personal situation, and I fear that it will continue to worsen and become more threatening without support from world public opinion.

Krimsky: Do you think the pressures increased after you received the Nobel Prize?

Sakharov: There have been other periods of intense pressure, such as in 1973. Just before receiving the prize, there was a quieter period. Possibly, they did not want to draw attention to me just before receiving the prize. It could have been that the let-up was a purely tactical move.

In general, I have constantly been under steady, heavy pressure for many years now.

The "incident in Omsk" related to the Sakharovs' attempt to attend the April 1976 trial there of Crimean Tatar spokesman Mustafa Dzhemilev. On April 17, shortly after his return to Moscow, Sakharov issued the following press statement on the trial and related events:

Dzhemilev's trial in Omsk proceeded in complete disregard of the law. Of Dzhemilev's sixteen friends and relatives, only four of his closest relatives were allowed into the courtroom. Later, two of those four were thrown out allegedly for disturbing the peace. The judge would not allow the defendant a final summation. Only two of his closest relatives were allowed to hear his sentencing. Throughout the trial, phone links between Omsk and Moscow were cut.

I will not discuss the substance of legal questions, of the judicial reprisals against an honest and courageous man nearly dead after a ten-month hunger strike and convicted on the basis of evidence extracted under duress from a witness who later retracted his testimony.

It was precisely that attempt to hide the illegality of what was happening in the courtroom that led to all the other lawbreaking.

I shall dwell only on one incident where my wife and I clashed with KGB agents in plain clothes, an event about which there has been a great deal of inaccurate foreign reporting I wish to clarify.

Using crude physical force, as they do at all political trials, the KGB prevented friends and relatives of the defendant from entering the courtroom. My wife and I were made special targets of this violence, so much so that I struck one or two KGB men and also one policeman whom the KGB ordered to push me aside.

I declare that my retaliatory actions—as well as my wife's—were not premeditated; they were an instinctive reaction to the violence, to the debasing treatment of Dzhemilev's friends and relatives, to the mockery of our laws, to the whole tragic circumstance of that trial and the other political trials in our country.

I wrote a statement at the police station in which I noted the illegal circumstances of the trial and apologized to the agents I hit. However, I also emphasized that in this case the police had sided with those who were breaking the law. My wife refused to submit any kind of written explanation.

The next day, after Dzhemilev's brother and sister were illegally evicted from the courtroom, my wife and I demanded an end to these continuing violations, and again we were shoved around. We were brought to the police station, where my wife insisted on receiving a medical examination; the examination disclosed widespread bruises—the direct result of the KGB's violence. We were treated properly at the police station, contrary to an initial report—distorted because it had to be transmitted in a roundabout way from Omsk.

I do not exclude the possibility of criminal proceedings being instituted against me. In such a case, the court will have to bring to light the main reason for the incident—the fact that KGB and court officials broke the law.

The two TASS articles on this incident are utter lies. One lie is that we allegedly started a fight with indignant citizens near the courthouse. But the principal lie is that we disturbed the peace and order inside the courtroom. We could have done no such thing for the simple reason that three ranks of KGB agents blocked us and the defendant's other friends and his relatives even from getting close to the courtroom—that is the heart of the matter.

A month after Mrs. Sakharov's return to Moscow from the trip abroad that began with her receiving medical treatment for her eyes in Italy and ended with her acceptance of her husband's Nobel Peace Prize in Oslo, a TASS article accused her of preparing "a filthy slander" against Soviet reality. According to the January 21, 1976, article ("Mrs. Bonner's Anti-Soviet Performance"), she was organizing a press appearance by Colonel Efim Davidovich, a Minsk "refusednik" and much-decorated war hero, in the Sakharov apartment, where he would "publicly renounce his motherland and all she has ever given him." Implying that Elena Bonner Sakharov's expenses in the West had been paid by others, the article said that "it is easy to explain the anti-Soviet activity which she took on with such zeal after her return. . . . Mrs. Bonner is now trying to pay off her thirty pieces of silver."

In a counter-statement the next day, Mrs. Bonner denied planning any "performance," noted that the apartment where they live is in fact her mother's, where Andrei Sakharov was not allowed to register as an official resident, observed that Colonel Davidovich had renounced the Soviet "state" but not his "motherland," and recalled that at least one Soviet newspaper had called the Nobel Prize "thirty pieces of silver." She added: "I cannot understand why the press of an atheistic state is so attached to Biblical references."

In a companion statement, Colonel Davidovich said the TASS attack "only proves one indisputable fact—that the bugging devices in the Sakharov apartment are not working properly. . . . the KGB knew that we had talked . . . but they could not figure out the sense of our conversation. Not wanting a reprimand from their superiors, the manufacturers of this Moscow 'Watergate' decided to make up a story. I never intended to renounce my homeland—the state of Israel—and the Soviet motherland already renounced me long ago by denying all I had done for the country in peacetime and at the front during the war. I traveled to Moscow to get the expert medical care I could not get in Minsk. . . ."

On March 1, 1976, Colonel Davidovich suffered five infarctions, or light heart attacks. On March 25, OVIR (the Office of Visas and Registration) refused to reconsider his request for permission to emigrate, and on April 24, he died. According to a statement Sakharov signed with fifty-six others, "He was murdered because he selflessly struggled for the right of Soviet Jews to emigrate to Israel and wholeheartedly defended every victim of persecution."

Russky Golos is a small Russian-language paper published in New York, whose editor holds the Soviet "Friendship of the Peoples" order, a decoration Moscow has given other Americans, including businessman Armand Hammer. Its article, "Madame Bonner—Sakharov's Evil Genius?," alleged that Mrs. Sakharov showed special favor to Zionist or Jewish dissidents and altered or modified some of her husband's public statements. Sakharov and some other members of the Academy of Sciences were mailed copies of the paper carrying this article.

Continuing his interview with George Krimsky, Sakharov described his private life and his dream of a "normal future":

Krimsky: I personally feel that your activity was more pronounced in some ways before you were awarded the Nobel Prize.

Sakharov: It was more what?

Krimsky: More pronounced. What I mean is that it was more noticeable, more active. It seems that during the past year there were fewer press conferences, fewer articles. Is that right?

Sakharov: I have given that very question a great deal of thought and I will try to answer it. First of all, generally speaking, one year is never the same as another. Chance occurrences differentiate one year from another. This past year has been a difficult one for our family personally. Besides that, I must admit that I am beginning to feel the strain after so many years of public activity for which I was psychologically ill prepared. It was psychologically very difficult for me to bear the burden of world fame, of all the meetings. Many of the meetings were completely useless, and they were extremely fatiguing. . . . All of this has an effect. Nevertheless, I do not feel that I have given up. I traveled twice to Omsk for Dzhemilev's trial and once to Nyurbakhan [where Tverdokhlebov was in Siberian exile —Ed.]. I released a great many documents on different subjects (close to thirty in five months); I can't say whether this was more or less than previous years—possibly it was somewhat less—but still there have been a great many. I write slowly and with great difficulty—I was definitely not meant to be a journalist. Each document costs me dear— sometimes a piece takes a few days, and sometimes a few weeks.

Some of the pieces I wrote during that period received widespread attention. One was my appeal to a U.S. Presidential candidate which received, as I understand it, extensive press coverage. But in other cases, the press took little notice of my documents and statements. This was especially true of radio coverage. And that helps create the impression that interest is waning.

I'll give you a few examples.

I wrote an appeal to a number of organizations, including the United Nations, to help Dzhemilev in his tragic plight. That statement virtually disappeared.

Another example is a statement made by my wife. She went to see Kuznetsov [in labor camp—Ed.] and found that he was then in the hospital. The authorities would not tell her how his health was, and they would not allow her to meet with him. They even said that her previous meetings had also been somehow illegal. In actual fact, according to the Soviet Code, they are completely legal and absolutely necessary, since there is no one else who can travel to see him. And yet her report also received no press or radio coverage.

I was very disturbed—I would say, almost unhinged—by what happened with one foreign newspaper correspondent's interview. We had agreed that I would submit answers in writing. I worked on them for two weeks and attached great importance to their complete, undistorted publication. But two weeks later, I was told that the newspaper wanted to print their own correspondent's article and not my answers. I took the piece back, and it has remained unpublished.

Krimsky: When was that?

Sakharov: It happened before the U.S. presidential elections. But I agreed to have it published later with a few minor changes.

I believe I have more or less answered your question.

On the one hand, I am always at work; on the other, I always have difficulties; it's all part of my life.

Krimsky: How much longer, may I ask, can your activity continue as it does now, considering your physical and psychological condition?

Sakharov: I really don't know. I live day by day, doing what life requires of me. How long that can continue depends on many factors, both personal and public. It depends in part on the help that I receive—on how younger men take on themselves the responsibility I carry, and in part on the support I get from world public opinion. It also depends, of course, on my health and on family matters.

When I reflect on what I want for my family and myself, then I must say that like every man I want a normal future, a normal life and destiny. But, unfortunately, in what is happening now, in this constant pressure we are all under, it is hard to see a happy ending. It is difficult to predict how things are going to turn out.

Krimsky: Your future. You have received several invitations to visit the West. Before, you have always said that you would not leave without permission to return. What do you think now, and where do you see yourself in another five years?

Sakharov: I shall now try to imagine, try to describe, my view of the situation. I have indeed received a great many invitations, including one to lecture at Princeton. Then, last year, I should have been able to receive the Nobel Prize in person. I always felt that I should be able to leave, that it would be rude to refuse such a trip, and impermissible in the case of the Nobel Lecture, but I naturally thought that I would be allowed to return to my country. I now see that my personal situation and my family's situation is getting worse year after year and could worsen even further. So, considering the past year's experience, I cannot seriously consider either a trip or permanent residence abroad as a way out of my personal situation; I believe that I must contemplate other alternatives for myself personally.

After Edward Kuznetsov's† "Prison Diaries" were published in Russian in the West, Mrs. Sakharov was interrogated by the KGB in November 1973, refusing to answer her interrogators but taking responsibility—in a November 20 public statement—for sending the manuscript to the West. Nevertheless, Gabriel Superfin† and Viktor Khaustov† were imprisoned for their involvement with the book.

Mrs. Sakharov had been able to visit Kuznetsov in prison and camp before 1976, taking the place of his invalid mother. Refused permission to see him in the Mordovian region camp hospital in November 1976—the occasion for her unnoticed public appeal—she and her husband made a lengthy, special visit to the settlement of Sosnovka, the administrative center of the Mordovian camps, in December 1977, in a second, unsuccessful attempt to have a family visit with Kuznetsov. At the same time he went on a hunger strike to protest being denied a meeting with them or with his wife (and co-defendant in the 1970 Leningrad hi-

jacking trial), Silva Zalmanson, who had been released from prison and allowed to emigrate to Israel.

In an interview for France-Soir, *February 23, 1977, Sakharov gave more details on his private life and life-style:*

Q: Tell me about your life: your salary, car, apartment, friends, what you read, what movies and theater you attend?

A: That is a very broad question, but I will begin with the last first. I have not been to the theater since early summer, 1975. At the urging of my friends, I did recently attend two concerts to hear [pianist Sviatoslav] Richter play Bach. Both concerts made an unforgettable impression on us; given the way we live, they seemed like a voyage into another world. I haven't been to a movie in a long time. I read very little. I have neither the time nor the strength for it. Sometimes before I go to sleep, I'll read English detective stories aloud to my wife. We allow ourselves such "relaxation" around two or three o'clock in the morning.

I have a fairly large income by Soviet standards: [every month] I receive 350 rubles as a senior scientific worker and 400 rubles as an Academician; my wife gets a pension of 120 rubles; my mother-in-law receives 85 rubles. That is our family's income. Our expenses are always greater. There are seven members in the family; we live together with my mother-in-law and with my stepdaughter's family in a two-room apartment to which I have no formal tie. My mother-in-law and Tanya's family felt cramped in the apartment and last year simply moved out of town to the *dacha*. The move greatly complicated their lives: my mother-in-law is unable to receive medical treatment, she sees no doctor at all; my grandson cannot go to nursery school; food, laundry, and other daily essentials are all a problem; on top of which, Tanya and Efrem are separated from their friends and their group. They are both jobless: Efrem has not been able to find work since he was fired in December 1975, and Tanya has two small children to take care of. Even if Efrem could find work, Tanya could not stay home alone in the *dacha* with two small children and an ailing grandmother. So, there are seven dependents in our family.

My son Dmitry is a student and I must support him. My brother is too ill to work, and the 120 rubles a month which I give him are his only income. My wife's son is also a student. He receives a 40-ruble stipend to which we add a little, and sometimes he earns more by giving lessons. His wife is also a student, receiving the same stipend, and they have a one-year-old daughter. I do not give any regular help to my married daughters. But we are constantly helping out friends, acquaintances, and strangers. And we live, as they say, forever "in hock." So much for my salary, or rather my income and expenses.

The question of our apartment is probably the major problem in our life. We had hoped to make an exchange which would let all seven of us live in one four-room apartment, but the borough executive committee, in violation of Soviet law, prohibited the swap. On March 2, the City Court will decide whether or not the borough court may hear our appeal against the borough executive committee's ruling.

A car? During working hours, but not on Saturdays and Sundays, I am allowed to request a car from the Academy of Sciences' garage. All Academicians have this right and, apparently, I can use an Academy car while I remain an Academician.

The complexities of swapping living quarters in the Soviet Union could fill a separate book. (In fact, The Ivankiad, a masterful satire of an actual exchange, has been written by Vladimir Voinovich and was published in the West in 1976.)

A typewritten letter warning Sakharov to stop speaking publicly and threatening death to Efrem Yankelevich and his son, Matvei, was put into the Sakharovs' mailbox late in 1975. The signature—"Central Committee of the Russian Christian Party"—is presumed to be an invention, but the threat itself was repeated to Yankelevich on a suburban street in January 1976, by two men who blocked his way home from a garbage dump. In the spring of 1976, Yankelevich's mother and an automobile mechanic to whom she had given her car for engine and rear-axle repairs were both interrogated by police in what seemed to be an attempt to prove that the car had been in an accident and Efrem had been driving it. Although his mother was told that a criminal case against him was being prepared, no charges were ever brought.

Tanya Semyonova Yankelevich was attacked in an article in Leninskoe Znamya (The Leninist Banner), *the Moscow Region Communist Party committee paper, as "the phantom laboratory assistant" in January 1977, and again in April in a Novosti press agency satirical piece distributed to foreign correspondents. From February to July she was also interrogated on several occasions about a supposed case of "group embezzlement of state property."*

In November 1977, the pressure turned from the Yankelevich family—they had left the Soviet Union—to Mrs. Sakharov's son, and on November 10, Sakharov called a press conference to issue an appeal for international concern:

I have called this press conference to report on a new, particularly serious form of pressure against our family. On November 5, my son, Aleksei Semyonov, was expelled on a false pretext from his fifth year at the Moscow State Lenin Pedagogical Institute. This occurred two months after his sister, Tanya Semyonova, and her husband, Efrem Yankelevich—the main targets of pressure against our family over the last two years—had left the Soviet Union, and nine months after the Procurator's Office of the USSR warned me to cease my public activity. The warning was to me, but it has been enforced against Tanya, Efrem, and now

Aleksei. The official reason for the expulsion was a report by the military training faculty on October 28. I will distribute copies of that report—clearly inspired from above.

That same day, the assistant rector of the Moscow State Pedagogical Institute, obviously subject to the same orders (indirectly or directly from the KGB, I am convinced), approved the expulsion order without verifying the true facts of the case. On November 5, the rector of the Institute signed the expulsion order.

Alyosha was one of the fastest-rising students in his year. He spent a great deal of time with those who had fallen behind. He successfully managed to work on several different pursuits—his studies, independent work, his time-consuming family obligations (his wife is also a student, and they have a three-year-old daughter, Katya)—and earned additional money by giving lessons at home.

The failing grade he received in his military course and the charge of systematically violating military discipline are manifestly the result of bias against him. I note this fact in my statement to the rector of the Moscow State Pedagogical Institute—copies of which I will distribute.

Before I give the floor to Professor Meiman* and then answer your questions, I would like in particular to stress that Alyosha Semyonov and his family are now nothing more than hostages with no prospects for the future at all. They must therefore try to leave the country, particularly since their situation could get considerably worse if Alyosha were drafted.

I appeal to the world public and particularly to student and scientific organizations to come out in active support of Aleksei Semyonov.

The documents Sakharov handed correspondents included the official pretext for the expulsion—the charge that by leaving camp four times "on his own accord" (serving five days in the guardhouse for the offense) and twice failing final examinations on military training, Semyonov had

---

* Mathematician Naum Meiman, a member of the Moscow Helsinki Watch Group, who has long sought permission to emigrate to join his daughter in the U.S.—Ed.

*demonstrated "moral and personal qualities" which made
him unfit to be a university teacher or student. In his protest to the institute's rector, Sakharov said his stepson had
been deliberately given a failing grade on an exam covering
material on which he had been earlier and successfully
tested and had left his unit because of his daughter's illness,
with a commander's oral permission and not during actual
study time. The prediction about emigration quickly proved
true. Semyonov applied to emigrate January 8, 1978, and
was told to pick up his exit visa four days later.*

*Repeatedly through 1976 and 1977, as the pressure on
him mounted, Sakharov was asked whether he, too, could
be forced to quit. Thus, this exchange with an interviewer
on October 30, 1976:*

Q: What do you now plan to do? Do you foresee a situation which would force you to ask to leave or even emigrate?

A: Up to now, my situation, like my family's situation,
has been worsening from year to year. It is conceivable that
it will continue to worsen in the future. I am hoping that
international public opinion will prevent such a development. I do not consider emigration or a temporary visit
abroad as a way out for myself personally.

*The same question, in a different form, was put by an
ABC News correspondent on March 25, 1977:*

Q: You are, no doubt, a source of constant irritation to
General Secretary Brezhnev. What has spared you, and
don't you fear for your personal safety or the safety of your
family?

A: I am concerned for my family's future. In 1973, international public opinion, my scientific colleagues in less
dangerous situations, supported and defended us. I am waiting now for that same support.

VII

Alarm and Hope

The following essay, completed March 7, 1977, was written at the request of the Norwegian Nobel Committee, for inclusion in an anthology the committee published in 1978. The original essay in Russian was published in 1977 by Khronika Press, New York.

> Injustice anywhere is a
> threat to justice everywhere.
> —Martin Luther King, Jr.

In all probability, my fellow authors in this anthology have stressed the grave and critical nature of our times. There is no need to enumerate once again the tragic problems of the modern world, foremost among them the threat of universal destruction in a major nuclear war. To a great extent these problems are created and aggravated by the division of humanity into opposing capitalist and socialist systems and into the Third World of developing countries.

It is widely acknowledged that the confrontation of the socialist and capitalist systems not only causes many of the difficulties the world faces but also affects the choice of possible resolutions for our most significant problems.

Over the past several decades—the greater part of its existence—the totalitarian-socialist system has been on a global offensive, constantly expanding its influence on mass psychology and political decisions in countries not formally affiliated with the system. The capitalist system has meanwhile been on the defensive. It is crucial to take this difference into account whenever such controversial issues as disarmament, ideology, and human rights are discussed. It is also important to recall the major changes that have recently occurred in this respect, known under the general heading of "relaxation of international tensions," as well as the truly substantial differences between the various socialist countries.

Expansionism in its most crude and predatory form was characteristic of Hitler's Germany. National Socialism, which brought disaster to many peoples and stained itself with monstrous crimes, lasted a total of twelve years until its ignominious end in 1945.

The totalitarian-socialist system which emerged almost thirty years ago in China after years of civil war represents a much more complicated and contradictory phenomenon. To its credit it has eliminated chronic famine which had cost millions of human lives in that vast and backward country. China is now apparently occupied predominantly with domestic problems. We know very little about the real life of the Chinese people and have no reason to hold illusions about it. In any event we do understand that the quality of material and spiritual life and of general economic development is still relatively low.

In conformity with China's low economic and military potential, foreign political activity is also minimal, being restricted almost completely to a struggle with the USSR for influence in developing nations, new Communist countries, and certain Communist parties. Of course, we cannot ignore the possibility of an about-face toward expansionism in the future based on a higher level of economic and military development. Given China's immense natural resources and population, such a turn of events could have extraordinarily serious circumstances. For the time being, however, it is no more than a future possibility.

The most refined form of totalitarian-socialist society exists in the USSR. The Soviet state's sixty-year history has been filled with horrible violence, hideous crimes at home and abroad, destruction, and the suffering, debasement, and corruption of millions of people. But especially in the early decades, this history also embraced great hopes, efforts to increase productivity, a spirit of dedication and sacrifice. Now all of this—the disgraceful and cruel, the tragic and heroic—has vanished under the façade of relative material well-being and mass indifference. A deeply cynical caste society has come into being, one which I consider dangerous (to itself as well as to all mankind)—a sick society ruled by two principles: *blat* (a little slang word meaning, "You scratch my back and I'll scratch yours"), and the popular saw: "No use banging your head against the wall." But beneath the petrified surface of our society exist cruelty on a mass scale, lawlessness, the absence of civil rights protecting the average man against the authorities, and the latter's total unaccountability toward their own people or the whole world, this dual irresponsibility being interrelated. As long as this situation continues, no one in our country, nor anywhere in the world, can allow himself to lapse into complacency.

But the danger that our injustice, our diseased bondage, could spread is not illusory. Along with countries now following its political line, the USSR wields substantial material and organizational strength. The USSR has succeeded in developing a strong, albeit unbalanced, economy on the bones of the Gulag slaves and through the ruthless exploitation of human and natural resources.

By channeling material and intellectual forces into the military sphere, the USSR has secured approximate military and technical parity with the more developed countries of the West, including major numerical advantages in tanks, submarines, artillery, and other areas. Of great significance is the USSR's possession of a powerful arsenal of missiles and nuclear weapons. The USSR has the largest peacetime army in the world. No less significant is the centralized and essentially militaristic structure of control over the economy, propaganda, transportation, communications, international trade, diplomacy, and so on.

But the main feature of this society is its "closed" nature. I use "closed" broadly to describe a system which blocks the majority of domestic information channels necessary for a democratic society. We are denied a free press;

it is almost impossible for the average citizen to travel abroad, difficult to emigrate and inconceivable to return.

It is precisely the society's "closed" nature which facilitates the nation's expansionist capabilities and simultaneously secures its antidemocratic stability despite failures, by Western standards, in satisfying social needs. Our standard of living is relatively low, particularly in housing, food, and clothing, and subject to wide variations from one region to another. The quality of education and health care is also low. The privileged minority enjoys vast advantages. But the Soviet citizen, having no basis for comparison, seems almost oblivious to all this, and the Westerner is totally unaware of many painstakingly concealed features of the system. His ignorance frequently leaves him defenseless against pro-Soviet propaganda, itself a form of expansionism. How a "closed" society works was demonstrated during the invasion of Czechoslovakia in 1968, when it proved a simple task to persuade most Soviet citizens to accept propaganda fables about the restoration of capitalism in that country, the German revanchist threat, and the like.

The most serious defect of a "closed" society is the total lack of democratic control over the upper echelons of the party and government in their conduct of domestic affairs and foreign policy. The latter is especially dangerous, for here we are talking about the finger poised on the nuclear button. The "closed" nature of our society is intrinsically related to the question of civil and political rights. The human-rights issue, therefore, is not simply a moral one, but also a paramount, practical ingredient of international trust and security. This thesis has been the leitmotif of my public statements over the last several years.

Marx and his disciples contended that the capitalist system had long ago exhausted its potential and that socialism's advantages in industrial organization, labor productivity, workers' living standards, and full citizen participation in all aspects of government would lead to the displacement of capitalism. Reality has proved otherwise. Socialism, at least in its totalitarian form, has indeed ex-

panded, but not at all because of its advantages and pro-
gressive nature.

Over the same period, the capitalist system has also
proved its capacity for development and transformation.
In countries of the West, a standard and "quality" of life
unprecedented in the history of mankind have been
reached; there have been great advances in social welfare.
Today's capitalist society, with a few reservations, can be
called "capitalism with a human face." The great achievements of science and engineering, which I view as the
root of this material progress, have created a profusion of
consumer goods which, in itself, has alleviated the problem
of the distribution of material wealth. But the *ideas* of
social justice, human rights, and democracy which have
permeated social consciousness—originating in Christianity
and other religious doctrines, and developing over the past
100–150 years through socialist thought, including Marxism
—play no less significant a role in capitalist society. We
can expect that over the next decade the West will make
progress in solving other problems as well—the depletion
of natural resources, population control, nationality questions, urban problems, crime, drug addiction, etc.—and will
do so democratically without mass restriction of personal
freedom.

We can also assume that socialist ideas, in their
pluralistic, anti-totalitarian form, will continue to play a
definite role in Western social development. This will in
fact be the movement of the West toward convergence
with the socialist world.

I feel less certain of a reciprocal evolution of totalitarian socialism toward pluralism. That will depend on
many internal and external conditions, the most important
of which is to overcome the "closed" aspect of totalitarian-
socialist society. Of course, these serious problems are not
instantly resolved. Inevitably, we will have to deal with
those who prescribe quick cures which are in fact more
dangerous than the disease. But in the democratic West,
with its wide-ranging, open discussion of critical issues,
the influence of such extremists will in the last analysis, I
hope, be neutralized.

In this respect, the evolution in the positions of a number of influential Western Communist parties is highly significant. For some time now, they have been moving away from pro-Soviet dogmatism toward classical social-democratic ideology.

Such are the prospects for the West if we ignore the context of confrontation with the socialist camp. But is the totalitarian order capable of independent, harmonious, and gradual development within its own frontiers? This system apparently requires expansion, informational isolation, and demagogic self-praise—particularly with respect to the "shining future" of its global historical mission—as well as the use of the fruits of the scientific and technical progress of the capitalism it attacks. Having encountered substantial difficulties both in domestic development and in relations with the outside world, the system's leaders have been finally forced to modify their tactics and appearances, although without initial changes in the system's ultimate goals. The original tactics, which could be called the "Comintern phase," went through several interim stages before being replaced by détente.

The term "détente" is not new; at one time (1933–39) it was used to define relations between Western countries and Hitler's Germany. I have no wish to suggest that détente is purely a trap for the West. Tactical changes have in fact acquired such substance that they have brought on important changes at deeper levels. It is especially important that détente opens new possibilities for mutual influence and a chance to lead humanity out of a difficult predicament, a chance which under no circumstances should be let slip. But détente carries with it a new danger, that totalitarian-socialist expansion has merely adopted a camouflage which makes it even more insidious.

What policy should the West adopt in its relations with the socialist countries under these new, more complex conditions? I am convinced that the main goal of détente is to guarantee international security. Essential to this goal are: disarmament, a strengthening of international trust, the surmounting of the closed nature of the socialist system, the defense of human rights around the world. These elements are not independent. Although disarmament occupies a certain priority, security cannot be attained by being limited to the purely military aspects of détente. Western leaders must not create the appearance of success in disarmament negotiations without real achievements; doing so, they would deceive their countries and—worst of all—provoke a unilateral disarmament. This danger is real because of both the tight secrecy in the socialist countries and the shortsightedness and domestic political maneuvering of certain Western politicians, who are prepared to jeopardize the delicate global balance for transitory political situations at home.

Disarmament negotiations are possible only from a position of equal strength. It is not only the West that is truly interested in disarmament and the USSR that compromises only in exchange for economic benefits, political and ideological concessions. In fact, the deeper interests of the USSR, gasping from overmilitarization, require decreases in military expenditures, and cutbacks in the army and in the military/industrial sector, to a much greater extent. In the actual conduct of diplomatic negotiations, it is essential to remember that the concept of disarmament has become central in Soviet propaganda; it cannot be ignored as easily as a trade agreement. Therefore, I believe the fear in the West that statements in defense of human rights may harm arms negotiations is unfounded.

Moreover, it is no less important to keep in mind that, without a true détente and the internal reform which it ideally requires, the actual scale of disarmament will be insignificant. The moral strength of the Western democratic tradition expresses itself in a calm, firm defense of human rights throughout the world. Supporting human rights in the socialist countries has the additional virtue of opening up the socialist system. Trade, scientific, and cultural contacts are important in their own right (especially for the socialist countries) as a means of continuing détente. But within reasonable limits they can also be used to bring indirect pressure toward reaching the basic goals of détente—disarmament and the guarantee of human rights.

I should like to spell out and enlarge on some of these ideas.

First of all—about disarmament. At the present time, there is much talk about limitations on strategic weapons as a first step on the path toward their reduction and toward an eventual total ban on all nuclear armaments. This discussion is urgent, since thermonuclear missiles already threaten the existence of civilization and will, in the future, threaten all live things on earth. Also, in a number of respects, the negotiations about these "overkill" weapons are turning out to be diplomatically and technically simpler. But with advances in engineering, technology, and mass production, conventional weapons now present a burgeoning danger. I have written on many occasions (in my Nobel Lecture, for example) that true international security must be based on a "balanced" disarmament where a "detailed parity" (a term borrowed from statistical physics) of all kinds of military forces is preserved at each stage between potential opponents. By this I mean a separate parity in tanks, military personnel, nuclear arms, aviation, and so on, in addition to parity in every strategic theater—in Europe, on the Sino-Soviet border, in the Indian Ocean, etc. Since each side will be tempted to try to maintain any advantage it has achieved and will at the same time try to catch up in areas where it lags behind, disarmament negotiations will be lengthy and complicated. But as long as negotiations, and not war, are under way, time is working for us—and "us" refers to all people living on this earth.

About human rights. Thanks to the efforts of many brave individuals, we know about the violation of human rights in the countries of Eastern Europe. In Czechoslovakia, which gave us an inspiring example of bold and desperately needed reforms in 1968, followed by the heroic nationwide resistance to the invasion by the USSR and its partners, a most important document—Charter '77—has been published. In Poland, we have seen the formation and successful struggle of the Workers' Defense Committee. The human-rights movement is developing in all countries of Eastern Europe. Its support is expanding because of the increasing section of the population outraged by the USSR's intolerable dictation of policy; its direction has been influenced by these countries' specific democratic and cultural traditions and by their historical position between East and West. The Roman Catholic Church has played an important role in these developments. In the USSR, the activity of the human-rights movement has taken new forms in the past several years: *samizdat* publication of *The Chronicle of Current Events,* a journal devoted to human-rights news; the Initiative Group to Defend Human Rights; the Moscow Human Rights Committee; the movements for the right to emigrate and the right to preserve national cultures (Jews, Germans, Ukrainians, Lithuanians, Estonians, Armenians, Georgians, Crimean Tatars, and others); and the Helsinki Watch Groups.

The entire world knows about the trials and extrajudicial oppression of human-rights advocates in the USSR and Eastern Europe. Reprisals are taken against loyal citizens for any expression of any opinion offensive to the authorities, including statements about the intolerably severe regimen in prisons and labor camps, about persecutions for religious activity, about illegitimate restrictions imposed on the freedom to choose one's country of residence or one's domicile within a country, or about other infringements of civil and political rights. The Universal Declaration of Human Rights, the International Human Rights Covenants, which today have the force of international law, and the Helsinki Final Act are the legal and political basis for the struggle against these intolerable violations.

I welcome the new, active stand adopted by some parliaments, governments, and heads of Helsinki Accord signatory states, in particular the position of President Jimmy Carter. Carter, with all the powers of his office and guided by the will of the American people, has proclaimed that the defense of human rights throughout the world is a moral obligation and cannot and should not interfere with other aspects of détente. This doctrine has great significance as a response to those who consider public statements and other actions in defense of human rights a threat to détente. I am convinced that it is possible and necessary to go further and make the struggle for human rights an essential element of all international relations, which will serve to ensure their practical success as well as their moral force.

The defense of prisoners of conscience, those who have sacrificed professional and personal interests and the welfare of their families for the sake of principle, deserves special attention in the framework of the struggle for human rights.

A worldwide political amnesty is a noble goal for the human-rights movement. In spite of the failure of the first attempt in 1975, public opinion should once again exert a maximum effort to have the UN make universal amnesty one of its goals.

The defense of human rights is not political in nature. It arises from moral principles and their link to peace. Therefore, all people of good will, whether their political opinions are "rightist" or "leftist," can and should participate in the defense of human rights. I am particularly pleased that trade unions and Communist parties in certain countries have begun to participate in this struggle—their involvement signals the effectiveness of the fight and the mass support it has developed.

As to the possible forms of pressure appropriate in securing human rights, we must bear in mind that a specific human-rights matter can be solved only when it has become a political problem for the leaders of a violator country. Détente creates various levers for exerting pressure which, without threatening to exhaust its potential, nonetheless brings specific human-rights questions as well as general problems to the attention of top policymakers. These levers are controlled not just by governmental and legislative bodies. There is a role for nongovernmental organizations and private citizens involved in exchanges—business firms, scientific associations, trade unions, workers, scholars, authors, and artists. I am not suggesting blackmail, of course, but rather the adjustment of interests which is a normal part of the process of eliminating confrontation. Such measures as a partial and temporary boycott of scientific or cultural contacts, temporary embargo on certain specialized equipment, or a dock workers' embargo do not threaten détente. Another example of a more general sanction is the Jackson-Vanik Amendment. Its goal is to prevent the violation of the crucial right to emigrate; since this is an amendment to the American law on trade, it cannot be deemed interference in the internal affairs of other countries or as a threat to détente.

Speaking of trade, industrial, and general economic relations, Soviet propaganda usually stresses their mutually profitable nature. These assertions should be analyzed with care. Of course, once a particular company or Western country has gotten a jump on its competitors, it may realize temporary benefits, but on the whole it is the USSR and the countries of Eastern Europe which are vitally interested in acquiring technology and credits. It will be totally unforgivable if the West fails to use this leverage to open up Soviet society.

I do, however, consider it morally impermissible to use food relief as a means of pressure. This comment does not extend to cases where such aid is used for speculative purposes or to stockpile reserves for possible military mobilization.

I also consider it intolerable to impose conditions on arms negotiations; they should have absolute priority.

The idea of an active defense of human rights is now embodied in an international ideology, articulated in many juridical documents and accords. Discussions on human rights have increased just as its advocates have multiplied. Human-rights questions have acquired a special urgency in the few months since President Carter and his new Administration proclaimed this principle as a key element of U.S. policy at home and abroad. Along with voices welcoming this stand, skepticism and even antagonism intensified. In particular, there was a negative official reaction in the socialist countries; the authorities cited the unacceptability of "interference in internal affairs" and backed up their position with an intensified campaign of harsh repression against dissenters, which directly challenged the U.S. position. In the West, the negative reactions have come either from shortsighted individuals who fail to understand the linkage between the defense of human rights and the problems of the world and of their own community, or else from people selfishly or politically interested in appeasing Soviet authority.

We are entering a critical period when the direction of international relations, the fate of countless victims of human rights violations, and the stability of détente and international security are at stake. In these circumstances, political leaders who have assumed responsibility for the fate of the world must demonstrate consistency, breadth, and courage in their decisions and a clear understanding of the situation.

Political leaders in the West should realize that any sign of weakness or inconsistency will seriously affect the fate of many people, among them dissenters in the USSR and Eastern Europe now absorbing the chief blows of repression. Unfortunately, political misjudgments have continued to occur and have resulted in grave consequences.

The leaders of the socialist countries, in their turn, should understand that common sense, the responsibility of their positions, world stability, and considerations of prestige all require that they take steps to respond to the demands of the entire world.

Dissenters demand respect for human rights, the development of democracy within the framework of the existing system, and the fulfillment of international undertakings; they reject violence on principle. Their voices do not reach the top decision-makers; their appeals are answered largely with repression. Therefore the Western public and its political leaders, when speaking with the leaders of socialist nations, in fact represent not only their own people, but also those who have been deprived of a voice in their own countries.

I have taken the words of Martin Luther King, Jr., winner of the Nobel Peace Prize, as the epigraph to this article. I believe they best express my thesis. Man's future depends on the energetic, public, and wise actions of people of good will everywhere who are inspired by moral principles. Lawlessness and infringements of human rights cannot be tolerated on this planet, any more than war, hunger, and poverty. The fate of each of us and all of us is at stake.

VIII

The World Outside

Sakharov's world is far broader than his family circle or his cramped housing. His concerns are also wider than the troubled world of Soviet dissent. As presented in interviews with journalists and two special essays collected in this chapter, his thoughts range from the tragedy of Lebanon to the hope of the SALT negotiations, from the moral controversy over capital punishment to the scientific one over peaceful nuclear power.

Two brief examples will illustrate the span of his thinking and expression. While the Palestinian refugee camp of Tel-Zaatar was under renewed siege from Lebanese Christian rightists in October 1976, Sakharov and his wife appealed together to the Secretary General of the United Nations, the heads of government of Security Council member states, and the President of Lebanon for urgent action:

The tragic situation of the wounded, children, and women in the besieged Palestinian camp of Tel-Zaatar requires immediate and decisive action. Use your great authority and influence to save the dying.

Over a year later, on November 4, 1977, Sakharov sent a short greeting to the opening of the Venice Biennale, an exposition devoted that year to the art and culture of dissent in Eastern Europe and the Soviet Union. Urging freedom of thought, conscience, and discussion as the best path to peace, he added:

In my field of science, the government's ideological interference is not open. The general anti-intellectual system is at work, however, in the decline of the tradition of education, in its militarization and bureaucratization, in the low living standards of the mass of the intelligentsia, in the total ideological deprivation of youth, through isolation from the milieu of world culture, and in nationalist and doctrinal discrimination. The situation is even worse in the arts and humanities, where all that is fresh and clear is rooted out and shriveled by the direct, undisguised pressure of the party and governmental ideological apparatus.

I hope that the Biennale will throw light on the full tragedy of creative life in the socialist countries and will simultaneously show that unofficial culture in the USSR and the countries of Eastern Europe nevertheless exists and grows, making its contribution to the free world culture mankind so much needs.

In his written responses on October 30, 1976, to the questions of an American journalist, Sakharov gave his overview of world issues:

Q: Which international events of the past year disturbed you specially?

A: In the past year the Western countries failed to take a decisive step toward working out a unified, long-term strategy for dealing with the socialist world and the developing countries. In particular, the European countries, it seems to me, still suffer from an anti-American prejudice, and that remains one obstacle to progress in this area.

The dangerous sluggishness in the disarmament negotiations is a direct result of the absence of such a strategy. With its eye on achieving a one-sided advantage, the USSR makes use of any diversion or vagueness in another country's policy.

War and force rule the world. The tragedy in Lebanon provides a graphic example of how a country, until very recently prosperous and enlightened, can be drawn into a bloody nightmare of force, murder, and destruction, as if it were being ravaged by an infectious illness.

While we condemn political adventurism, anti-Semitism, and the international crimes perpetrated by Palestinian extremists, at the same time we have no right to condone the genocide practiced against the Palestinians —to act as if this people did not exist. Several weeks ago my wife and I made a public appeal in defense of the women, children, and wounded in the besieged Palestinian camp of Tel-Zaatar, and our concern extends to all who are victims of military actions. In Angola, we see the population fighting as guerrillas against the civil-war victors, against marauding, hungry Cuban soldiers, against punitive expeditionary forces. These are the tragic consequences of the terrible situation in all southern Africa. Here again, the Soviet Union, following traditional policies in the Near East and in many other trouble spots, is against compromise, against realistic alternatives for peaceful settlement. Can it be that, once again, the world cannot summon the strength to withstand chaos?

A year and a half after the end of the war in Vietnam it is impossible to forget about the millions of victims allegedly killed in Cambodia. No one knows for certain what is happening in what was South Vietnam—it is only evident that all is not well there; it is no happenstance that each month hundreds of refugees risk their lives to escape from that country. The Western public that actively sought to bring an end to the war in Vietnam must now show its concern for the fate of the people in that part of the world.

A majority of countries have witnessed the expansion of international terrorism, that most dangerous breach of international stability and of the fundamental laws of human morality. I cannot but recall here the elation produced by the Israeli commandos' fantastic rescue operation at the Ugandan airport in Entebbe.

But in speaking about terrorism, I must not pass over my own condemnation of those Jewish extremists who committed terrorist actions against Soviet organizations in the U.S. and in other countries (although I completely share their indignation at certain aspects of Soviet policy).

In choosing the path of terrorism, these people in fact do great damage both to Soviet Jews and to all struggles for human rights, which have consistently and fundamentally adhered to nonviolent methods.

Another issue on my mind concerns the reports of a campaign in Israel to deny help to people who intend to emigrate from the USSR, but do not wish to go to Israel. Taking into account the obstacle to emigration from the USSR, the history of the fight for the right to emigrate, and the fact that the emigration problem falls inside the human-rights issue as a whole, I view this campaign with real misgivings.

On February 10, 1977, a CBS interviewer questioned Sakharov about the connection or "linkage" between human rights and nuclear disarmament accords:

Q: How does the human-rights campaign influence disarmament and the search for agreement on limiting strategic weapons?

A: Let me illustrate that point with one example. The biologist Sergei Kovalev is on the verge of death in Perm Labor Camp No. 36. This amazing man was present at the birth of the human-rights movement in our country and is one of the editors of *The Chronicle of Current Events,* a publication which most graphically and clearly depicts how the human-rights movement strives toward openness and truth in our society. Kovalev is terribly ill with a malignant tumor. Only an operation can prolong his life. For a year now we have tried in vain to get him transferred to the Leningrad prison hospital.

If, under pressure from world public opinion, Kovalev is finally transferred to the hospital,° is it possible that the SALT talks will be threatened? If that should indeed be the case, we would see how much all the Soviet assertions of their commitment to disarmament are really worth. In answer to those who warn that the human-rights struggle will have a ruinous effect on other aspects of détente and

---

° He was transferred and successfully operated on in March. See Chapter II.

linkage

particularly on the disarmament negotiations, President Carter recently stated his determination to regard these two issues as separate. I welcome the President's statement, and I want to add that as a matter of fact the fundamental struggle for human rights greatly strengthens the position of the West. It promotes international trust, without which there can be no international security. In the best way, it fosters personal contacts among the leaders of countries and thereby creates an opportunity to conduct a productive dialogue in relatively less complex fields. It furthers the general humanization of the USSR and the Eastern European countries while at the same time making them more secure and engendering confidence. But most important, it further strengthens the moral and ethical position of the West:

As Secretary of State Vance was beginning his first round of SALT talks, an ABC News interview on March 25, 1977, elicited from Sakharov a clarification of his thinking on linkage:

Q: Cyrus Vance is hoping for success in the negotiations. Do you think that the Soviet side will negotiate more stubbornly because of President Carter's support for the dissidents?

A: I, too, hope that the negotiations will be successful and that the Soviet leaders will act responsibly and in good faith. President Carter has asserted the view that disarmament and human rights are separate and independent issues. That is a good answer to those who oppose an active defense of human rights out of fear of endangering détente.

In fact the Soviet Union must certainly be as interested in disarmament, trade, and scientific contacts as is the West, and I think that the Soviet leaders are ready to accept the principle of considering complex problems separately and are prepared to conduct the negotiations in a businesslike manner, despite their tough public statements protesting supposedly inadmissible, improper interference in their internal affairs. Look, the negotiating stances are part of a verbal duel in themselves. The West must remain calm in the face of these harsh polemics, articles in the Soviet press, etc., and stick to its basic line both in regard to human-rights questions and in regard to disarmament.

In this respect, it is true that separate treatment of these problems is expedient in a tactical sense, but in the final analysis it is impossible to achieve international security and trust without first overcoming the closed nature of Soviet society, i.e., without solving the human-rights problem. Though it is possible to keep cool during the verbal duel, it is nonetheless impossible to stay calm when the elementary rights of real people are trampled. The recent arrests of members of the Helsinki Watch Groups—Ginzburg,† Orlov,† Rudenko,† Tykhy,† Shcharansky†—demand energetic protest. [See Chapter X.—Ed.]

After Secretary Vance left Moscow with the SALT talks at an angry impasse, Sakharov told an interviewer from the Swedish/Norwegian radio and television network on April 4, 1977, that the negotiating problem was one of military power, not human rights:

Q: How do you evaluate the outcome of the U.S. Secretary of State's negotiations in Moscow?

A: I see the negotiations between Secretary of State Vance and the Soviet leaders as a necessary stage in the complex and contradictory development of relations between our countries. In the course of the negotiations, as far as I can understand, possibilities arose for progress in such areas as the Near East and a comprehensive nuclear-test ban, as well as on some other issues. But most important is the fact that Vance made a U.S. proposal to limit and reduce the number of strategic weapons. If it is developed further, this could potentially open the way to keep this dangerous area of rivalry out of future superpower relations.

For the present, the Soviet leaders have turned the

American proposal down, but I do not think that this diminishes the significance of the fact that at least one side made an important step forward.

Q: Why did the Soviet government reject the American proposal on limiting strategic weapons?

A: The Soviet government's decision caused a great deal of anxiety all over the world. Soviet Foreign Minister Gromyko, in a press-conference statement, tried to explain Soviet motives for rejection of the U.S. proposal and made countercharges against the new U.S. Administration. What, then, in my opinion, actually took place?

Above all, the U.S. position on human rights is in no way to "blame." The reason for the rejection, according to Gromyko's statement to the press, lies at the heart of the problem. In short, the Soviet leaders do not want to lose the essential strategic advantage established in the formulations agreed upon in Vladivostok. As is well known, the basic strength of Soviet missile power lies in the fact that their rockets have two and one half to three times more throw-weight than do analogous American rockets. The Vladivostok agreement made no provision or compensation for this significant advantage to the USSR. And I think that the U.S. attempt to reopen this unsolved problem was precisely the major reason for the Soviet leaders' reacting so negatively to the American proposal.

For the sake of preserving a strategic balance in the world, Vance sought either to cut the number of the Soviet Union's most powerful rockets by half and simultaneously to make an equivalent decrease in the number of American rockets and put a limit on the operational radius of cruise missiles, or, alternatively, to keep the essentials of the Vladivostok agreement intact but allow unlimited strategic use of cruise missiles as compensation for the one-sided Soviet throw-weight advantage over the U.S. I will not go into further details, but I consider the American proposal a sensible one. It opens the way to eventual curtailment of the arms race. True disarmament is possible only when neither side insists on having superiority, but the Vladivostok agreement afforded the USSR just such an advantage.

Q: How do you assess the prospects for future negotiations on limiting and reducing strategic weapons?

A: The agreements the USSR concluded in the last years concerning disarmament questions, including Vladivostok, do evidence a certain departure from extremist policies of militarization and expansionism. This development permits one to hope that the continuation and deepening of the new American Administration's policy, given united support—public and governmental—by all the Western countries, will bring the desired positive results in the disarmament and human-rights fields and in other areas as well. We have to be ready to accept the fact that the road, in all probability, will not be as straight as we would like. In particular, there is no way to rule out the possibility that the West will sometime have to apply added strength in order to achieve a strategic balance, as an essential prerequisite for successful disarmament negotiations.

In the fall of 1977, Sakharov was invited to address the Amnesty International Conference on the Abolition of the Death Penalty. Barred from foreign travel, he composed the following statement on September 9 for delivery to the December meeting in Stockholm:

I am grateful for the invitation to take part in a symposium on the abolition of the death penalty, a subject which has been a matter of concern to me. Since I am unable to go to Stockholm, I submit this letter as my statement to the Conference.

I fully support the basic arguments advanced by opponents of the death penalty.

I regard the death penalty as a savage, immoral institution which undermines the ethical and legal foundations of a society. The state, in the person of its functionaries (who, like all people, are prone to superficial judgments and may be swayed by prejudice or selfish motives), assumes the right to the most terrible and irreversible act— the taking of human life. Such a state cannot expect an improvement in its moral atmosphere. I reject the notion that the death penalty has any real deterrent effect what-

soever on potential criminals. I am convinced that the contrary is true—that savagery begets only savagery.

I deny that the death penalty is in practice necessary
or effective as a means of defending society. The temporary isolation of offenders which may be necessary in
some cases must be achieved by more humane and more
flexible measures which can be rectified in the event of
judicial error and adjusted to take account of changes in
society or in the personality of the offender.

I am convinced that society as a whole and each of its
members individually, not just the person who comes before the court, bears responsibility for the occurrence of a
crime. No simple solutions exist for reducing or eliminating
crime, and in any event, the death penalty provides no
answer. Only a gradual evolution of society, a growth of
humanitarian attitudes which lead people to a deep respect
for life and human reason and a greater concern for the
difficulties and problems of their neighbors, can reduce
crime or eliminate it. Such a society is still no more than a
dream. Only by setting an example of humane conduct today can we instill the hope that it may someday be
achieved.

I believe that the principle involved in the total abolition of the death penalty justifies disregarding those ob-
jections which are based on particular or exceptional cases.

While still a child, I read with horror the remarkable
collection of essays *Against the Death Penalty* published
in Russia with the participation of my grandfather I. N.
Sakharov in 1906–1907 during the wave of executions following the 1905 revolution. I have read the impassioned
statements of Tolstoy, Dostoevsky, Hugo, Korolenko,
Rozanov, Andreyev, and many others. From the above-
mentioned collection I know the arguments of a number of
scholars: Soloviev, Bazhenov (the psychology of condemned persons), Gernet, Goldovsky, Davydov, and
others. I share their conviction that the psychological
horror associated with the death penalty renders it dispro-
portionate to the vast majority of crimes and inappropriate
as a just retribution or punishment in every case. And indeed, how can one speak of the punishment of a person

who has ceased to exist? I share their conviction that the death penalty lacks any moral or practical justification and represents a survival of barbaric customs of revenge—cold-blooded and calculated revenge, with no personal danger for the executioners, with no passionate personal involvement on the part of the judge, and therefore shameful and disgusting.

I must comment briefly on the widely discussed subject of terrorism. I am of the opinion that the death penalty is completely ineffective in the struggle against terrorism and other political crimes committed by fanatics. In such cases the death penalty serves only as a catalyst for the psychosis of lawlessness, revenge, and savagery. I do not in any way sanction the current phenomenon of political terrorism, which is often accompanied by the death of random persons, by the taking of hostages (including children), and by other dreadful crimes. I am convinced, however, that imprisonment (possibly reinforced by the adoption of a law forbidding release before completion of sentence in cases specified by the court) is a more rational measure for the physical and psychological isolation of terrorists and for the prevention of further acts of terror.

The abolition of the death penalty is especially important in a country like ours with its unrestricted state power, its uncontrolled bureaucracy, and its widespread contempt for law and moral values. You know of the mass executions of innocent people which were carried out during the 1930s and 1940s in a mockery of justice, not to mention the still greater numbers who perished without any legal proceedings at all. We are still living in the moral climate created during that era.

I wish to stress the fact that in the USSR the death penalty is a possible punishment for many crimes which have no relation to crimes threatening human life. You may recall, for example, the case of Rokotov and Faibishenko, who were charged in 1961 with underground traffic in gems and illegal currency operations. After they had been sentenced to imprisonment, the Presidium of the Supreme Soviet passed a law which extended application of the death penalty to large-scale crimes against property. Rokotov and

Faibishenko were retried and sentenced to death in violation of the fundamental legal principle barring retroactive application of criminal sanctions. Many other persons have since been executed under analogous laws, essentially for carrying on private business activities. In 1962 an old man was shot for counterfeiting a few coins which he had buried in his yard.

The total number of executions in the USSR is not known; the statistics are a state secret. But there are grounds to believe that several hundred persons are executed annually, a greater number than in most countries where this barbaric institution persists. Other aspects of our life must be taken into account in any discussion of capital punishment in the USSR: the backward and dismal condition of our criminal justice system, its subservience to the state machine, the prevalence of bribery and corruption, and the frequent interventions of local big shots in judicial procedures.

I receive a great many letters from persons convicted of crimes. I cannot check the facts in every case, but taken all together, these letters create an irrefutable and terrible picture of lawlessness and injustice, of superficial and prejudiced investigation, of the impossibility of obtaining review of clearly mistaken or dubious verdicts, of beatings during police questioning.

Some of these cases involve death sentences. Here is one such case. I have before me a copy of the court verdict in the case of Rafkat Shaimukhamedov,† documents on his case prepared by lawyers, letters by his mother. On May 31, 1974, in Issyk-Kule, Shaimukhamedov, a worker and by nationality a Tatar, was sentenced to be shot. He had been convicted of murdering a female shop assistant—while intending to commit robbery along with two accomplices. (The latter were sentenced to several years' imprisonment.) Shaimukhamedov denied his guilt, refused to ask for pardon, and declared a hunger strike. He passed twenty months in the death cell expecting either execution or a review of his case. Throughout this time his mother and lawyers submitted dozens of complaints, but all higher authorities sent them back without any examination of the matter. In January 1976 the sentence was carried out with the sanction of Deputy Procurator General of the USSR Malyarov.

The court verdict on Shaimukhamedov is striking for its illiteracy, in both the literal and the juridical sense of the word, given its lack of proofs and its contradictory nature. An even more vivid picture emerges from the complaints of the lawyers and the mother's letters. The convicted persons' presence at the scene of the crime was not proved. The court ignored the contradictory versions of the accusation, the testimony of witnesses, and the facts of the expert examination (according to which the victim's blood group did not match that of a spot of blood found on Shaimukhamedov's clothing). The mother's letters state that the reason for this bias lay in the selfish material interest of two procurators (Bekboev and Kleishin). She describes scenes of extortion, bribes received by them from another accused, the fabrication of a criminal case against her second son with the same goal of extortion—even after the shooting of Rafkat. I cannot verify these reports, but to me the main message is clear: with what ease and absence of argument the death penalty was passed, and how easily so terrible a case becomes routine.

I have dwelt on this case in detail because it seems to me that it clearly reflects the complete horror of the death penalty and its destructive effect on society.

I hope that this symposium will make a contribution to the noble effort of many generations toward the complete abolition of the death penalty throughout the world.

If Sakharov's views on capital punishment generally fit within the Western liberal canon, his vigorous advocacy of the development of nuclear power does not. The following article was written at the invitation of Professor Frantisek Janouch, formerly head of the theoretical nuclear physics department at the Nuclear Research Institute in Prague. Now working in Stockholm, Professor Janouch has also been a proponent of nuclear energy and solicited his Soviet colleague to comment in the continuing scientific and political debate. Sakharov's reply was received in December 1977 and printed in the June 1978 issue of The Bulletin of the Atomic Scientists, *under the author's title, "Nuclear Energy and the Freedom of the West."*

One often hears on the radio or reads in the press about demonstrations involving thousands of people, about speeches by well- or lesser-known statesmen, about various campaigns in the Western countries—all directed against the development of nuclear energy production, against construction of nuclear power stations, breeder reactors, etc. Although I have been rather amazed by this and even somewhat indignant, for a long time I restrained myself from any public statement, especially since, naturally, nothing of this kind takes place in the USSR. Gradually, however, I came to the conclusion that this subject deserves attention and that I have something to say about it.

The basic reason for antinuclear feelings among people is probably the fact that they do not have sufficient information about the complex and very specialized problems involved. Due to this lack of information, the natural and legitimate concern of contemporary man for preservation of his environment is misdirected.

It is difficult to explain to a nonspecialist (although it is actually true) that the nuclear reactor of a nuclear power station is nothing like an atomic bomb, that the power station burning coal or oil offers much greater danger and harm to the environment, as well as a biological threat to the people, than does an atomic station or breeder reactor of the same capacity rating.

Many responsible statesmen of the West, industrial leaders, and nuclear scientists have now come to understand (though belatedly) that it is necessary to bring the basic technical facts to the attention of the public. They now understand the need for large-scale scientific and technical propaganda. This is truly very important. Hans Bethe, Nobel laureate in physics, wrote an excellent, well-argued article, "The Necessity of Fission Power," which was published in *Scientific American* in January 1976. He is the author of theoretical works on thermonuclear processes in the stars, on quantum electrodynamics and nuclear physics. European readers probably know also the name of Professor Janouch, who has repeatedly expressed himself on the same subject.

I am in complete accord with the reasoning of these and many other authoritative writers.

The development of nuclear technology has proceeded with much greater attention to the problems of safety techniques and preservation of the environment than the development of such branches of technology as metallurgy, coke chemistry, mining, chemical industry, coal power stations, modern transportation, chemicalization of agriculture, etc. Therefore, the present situation in nuclear power is relatively good from the point of view of safety and possible effects on the environment. The ways to improve it further are also quite clear. The basic peculiarity which distinguishes nuclear technology from that using chemical fuels is the high concentration and small volume of the dangerous by-products and also the small size of the process as a whole. This makes it easier to solve the safety and environmental problems for a nuclear power station than it is for a power station using coal, oil, etc.

At the same time it is obvious that it is necessary to force the pace of development of nuclear technology, since it is the only economically feasible method—available in the next few decades—of replacing the use of oil (which, according to most estimates, will become both too expensive and scarce by the end of the century because of the exhaustion of convenient deposits and increased extraction costs). Moreover, it is very important not only to construct "conventional" atomic power stations working on enriched uranium, in which the rare uranium isotope U-235 is used, but also to solve the problem of producing fissionable material from the main uranium isotope and eventually from thorium.

This will make it economically feasible to utilize poor uranium ores, large deposits of which are found in the earth's crust. Later this will make it possible to utilize thorium ores, the deposits of which are even more abundant. As is well known, fast-neutron reactors (breeders) are only one of the possible solutions of this problem. Both their engineering design and the development of safety measures are well advanced. Apparently, in the near future it will become necessary to start building industrial fast-neutron reactors. Naturally, maximum attention to safety measures will be called for.

I have already written about one possible alternative solution to the problem of producing fissionable materials, and I would like to mention it here. (I have also emphasized that I am not the originator of this idea.) I am speaking about a proposal to build a large underground chamber (probably with a hermetically sealed, heatproof, corrugated shell) in which explosions of especially prepared thermonuclear charges of minimal power are caused to occur periodically. The products of such explosions are subsequently withdrawn from the chamber and processed. With charges of this kind, very effective production of fissionable material can be attained by letting the neutrons from the thermonuclear reaction be absorbed by uranium or by thorium. Of course, attractive as this idea is, there are many serious difficulties in its implementation.

One other problem much discussed in the literature is the possible theft of fissionable materials from a power station or from a reprocessing plant. The stolen materials could be used to produce a primitive atomic bomb. As far as the possibility of theft is concerned, I think that by proper organization and technical security measures, such a possibility will be made minimal. Besides, one can hardly envy the thief who would dare to steal a fuel rod from a nuclear reactor; most likely he himself will perish and the plutonium contained in one rod will not be sufficient to produce an atomic bomb. As far as producing a "do-it-yourself" atomic bomb is concerned, I am bound by security regulations, as Hans Bethe evidently is. However, like Bethe, I can assure readers that this is a very complex procedure, not easier than, for example, building a "do-it-yourself" space rocket. In addition, one can assume that obtaining a critical mass will be handicapped by the denaturing of plutonium and other fissionable materials with neutron-active additives.

The whole problem of nuclear energy production

should be considered from more than just the economic and technical points of view. In the rest of this article, I want to discuss the international and political implications of this problem. When I had already started working on this article, I happened to hear on the radio a broadcast about a book by an English astrophysicist, Fred Hoyle. I have not read this book, but judging from the broadcast, Hoyle's point of view and his apprehensions are close to mine.

Policymakers always assume, not without reason, that one of the many factors in determining the political independence of a country, its military and diplomatic strength, and its international influence is the level of economic development of the country and its economic independence. This assumption is doubly valid in the case of two world systems opposing each other. But the level of a country's economy is determined by its energy technology—that is, by the utilization of oil, gas, and coal at present; of uranium and thorium in the near future; and perhaps of deuterium and lithium in the more distant future, when the very complex technical problems of controlled thermonuclear synthesis will have been solved. Therefore I assert that the development of nuclear technology is one of the necessary conditions for the preservation of the economic and political independence of every country—of those that have already reached a high stage of development as well as of those that are just developing. For the countries of Western Europe and Japan, the importance of nuclear technology is particularly great. If the economy of these countries continues to be in any important way dependent on the supply of chemical fuels from the USSR or from countries which are under her influence, the West will find itself under constant threat of the cutting off of these channels. This will result in a humiliating political dependence. In politics, one concession always leads to another, and where it will finally lead is hard to foresee.

I have already had an opportunity to tell in *My Country and the World* about a statement of an important Soviet official which I heard in 1955 when I still could be considered "one of the boys." He was talking about the reorientation of Soviet policy in the Near East, about the support of Nasser in order to create an oil crisis in Western Europe and thus obtain an effective lever for exerting pressure there. Now the situation is much more complex and full of nuances. But some parallels undoubtedly exist. There is a political interest on the part of the USSR in exploiting energy shortages in the West.

Is the present campaign against the development of nuclear power inspired by the USSR (or other countries of Eastern Europe)? I know of no reliable facts supporting this. If it were so, then insignificant and indetectible efforts are sufficient to influence substantially the dimensions of this campaign because of widespread antinuclear prejudice and lack of understanding of the inevitability of the nuclear era.

I must end this article on the same note on which I started it. People must have the opportunity, that is, the knowledge, and the right to consider the mutually connected economic, political, and ecological problems involved in the development of nuclear power, as well as the problems involved in alternative ways of economic development. And they must consider these issues soberly and responsibly, without unfounded emotions and prejudices. What is involved here is not just comfort, or preservation of the so-called quality of life, but the much more fundamental problem of economic and political independence, and the preservation of freedom for their children and grandchildren. I am sure that in the end a proper decision will be reached.

IX

Official Brutality

Sakharov's position in Soviet society is an extraordinary anomaly. Revered as a physicist, he is scorned by the political and police authorities and yet sought out continually by ordinary people with grievances the system has not addressed or resolved. Over the years of his public activity, he has played a continuing role in attracting world attention to otherwise anonymous individuals, hoping that his celebrity could give them a measure of protection and help. In 1975 and 1976, however, he became deeply disturbed by the mysterious deaths of two such visitors—both of whom were apparently killed shortly after leaving his apartment —and by the evidence that dissidents in small, faraway towns were also being killed or driven to their deaths.

Written October 30 in Moscow, his address to the Second Sakharov Hearing*—held in Rome, November 25– 28, 1977—brings together many of his specific continuing concerns, introduces his hopes for the Helsinki process, and repeats the call he made after the Moscow subway explosion for a full investigation of the unexplained deaths:

I want to take advantage of this opportunity to express a few thoughts on the subject of human rights in the USSR and the countries of Eastern Europe. I call upon the commission:

* The Hearings Commission heard the public testimony of approximately twenty witnesses from the Soviet Union, Czechoslovakia, East Germany, Poland, Bulgaria, and Romania before resolving that it had heard enough evidence—except about Romania—to denounce the violation of fundamental human rights in those countries and the consequent contravention by them of international human-rights agreements.

1. To investigate reports of the violation of human rights and international standards in places of imprisonment—intolerable conditions of forced labor; restrictions on prisoners' diets, meetings, correspondence; arbitrary and harsh punishment; torture by cold and hunger; and the denial of other rights—through the depositions of eyewitnesses, written and oral testimony, and official documents, the Corrective Labor Code in particular. The investigation of these violations must cover political as well as criminal offenders.

2. To demand an investigation of the criminal offenses committed against dissidents and other opposition groups, including representatives of religious sects, which have not been officially investigated fully and openly. I refer particularly to the cases of Biblenko,† Bogatyrev,† Brunov, Lukshaite,† Tamonis,† Deinega,† Shkraba†—all of whom were killed under unknown circumstances—and to the cases of Kryuchkov and Likhachov—who were assaulted and beaten.

3. To investigate reports of the massive lawlessness used against those Crimean Tatars who returned to the Crimea in 1967–77 and were denied residence permits, exiled, assaulted, beaten, had their houses destroyed, were refused jobs or admission to schools, were subjected to judicial repression, suffered confiscation of their goods, and so forth.

4. To investigate instances of discrimination in education and employment on national grounds, on account of peasant background, because of religious beliefs or previous convictions, and for other reasons.

5. To investigate the protection of workers' rights—the lack of the right to strike, the problem of guaranteeing workers fair pay and social status—citing the Soviet press and testimony of eyewitnesses.

6. To investigate the violation of religious freedoms, the prohibition against all forms of religious propaganda, the anti-church character of state control over religion, the prohibition of church charitable work, discrimination against believers, the denial of parental rights to believers whose children are forcibly taken away to prevent their being

raised in a religious faith, as well as other forms of force and illegality directed against believers and the repression of religious groups which reject what they consider anti-ecclesiastical forms of state control. The persecution of the True Orthodox Church, Baptists, Seventh Day Adventists, Pentecostals, Uniates, and others should be included here.

7. To investigate the problem of free emigration and of travel abroad to visit relatives, obtain medical care, study, work, and tour. . . .

8. To investigate violations of the free flow of information.

9. To investigate the misuse of psychiatry for political purposes. The special hospital "Sytchevka," according to the materials prepared by Iosif Terelya, can be cited as an example of an especially severe violation of human rights and common decency.

The persistent and protracted violation of fundamental civil liberties and human rights in the USSR and the countries of Eastern Europe has brought a definite change in the psychology of people in general and of the intelligentsia in particular. For that reason those groups and individuals who have decided to analyze events in their societies for themselves and have broken with the norm of resigned silence about all which is negative play an extraordinarily important role. By themselves they are establishing the conditions for the restoration of a healthy civic consciousness and life. . . . But the harshest, most illegal repression is most often directed precisely at these groups and people. In urging international protection of human rights as a necessity, we must give special consideration to these groups and people.

10. I urge you to use publications and witnesses' depositions, to collect information on the situation and illegal treatment of all prisoners of conscience, and to demand their release. . . .

The Sakharov Hearings are taking place during the Belgrade Meeting, and this increases their significance. I think that the materials of the hearings should be sent to the conference and also published in the press. I hope that the work of the hearings will focus attention on the violation of human rights in the USSR and Eastern Europe and will contribute to correcting that situation. It is very important that the hearings be made a continuing process, that they convene periodically, and that a permanent working commission be established to collect materials.

By defending human rights wherever they are being violated we protect all humanity and ensure our common future.

Two deaths which haunted Sakharov were those of men from outside Moscow who had come there to ask him for help. The first was that of Evgeni Viktorovich Brunov, who died the night of November 5–6, 1975, on his way home by train to Klin after a talk with Sakharov, who had escorted the thirty-seven-year-old jurist to the railroad station. His body, with a crumpled photograph of Sakharov in his clothes, was found beside the railroad tracks, and his death was officially attributed to a fractured skull. His mother, however, has said that witnesses told her Brunov had been thrown from the train by unidentified persons. Since 1968, when he wrote a letter protesting the Soviet invasion of Czechoslovakia, Brunov, according to his mother, had been persecuted by the KGB and forcibly confined twelve times in psychiatric hospitals. Sakharov received no response to his inquiry regarding the "Brunov affair," or to his proposal that the testimony of witnesses be taken.

The second death occurred even closer to home, although Sakharov did not mention it in his address to the hearings. On the afternoon of March 25, 1977, Aleksandr Fyodorovich Yakovlev, a driver from Novosibirsk, came to tell Sakharov of a job-related injustice he had suffered. Like many such visitors, Yakovlev had come at the suggestion of his co-workers, who advised him to turn to Sakharov for help in getting back the job he had lost for refusing to fix the garage head's private car. Around six o'clock—a couple of hours after Yakovlev left—his mother arrived at the apartment weeping and explaining that she had been waiting for her son near the Kursk railroad station (less than half a mile from the Sakharovs') but that he had never shown up. Sakharov joined in a search that lasted until April 1, when Yakovlev's mother telephoned to say that she had found her son's body at the Balashikha morgue outside Moscow and had been told that he had been killed in a hit-and-run accident on the Sadovoye Koltso (Garden Ring), the street on which both the Sakharov apartment and the Kursk station are located. Police, however, said no accident had happened on that extremely busy main thoroughfare, a fact confirmed by a number of street vendors working in the area. Moreover, although Yakovlev's mother had been told her son's body carried no identification and was brought to the Balashikha morgue for that reason, Yakovlev had been carrying his work papers and had shown them to Sakharov, and the Sakharovs were told at the morgue on April 4 that unidentified bodies are never brought there from Moscow. It should be pointed out that, in contrast to the "Brunov affair," there is no known documentation available concerning the death of Yakovlev.

Two victims of beatings were Nikolai Nikolaevich Kryuchkov, a young man who had sought to emigrate from the USSR to America; and Dmitri Sergeevich Likhachov, at seventy one of the most distinguished Soviet scholars of ancient Russian literature.

Kryuchkov had been forcibly committed to the Kashchenko Psychiatric Hospital in May 1974, before President Nixon's second visit to Moscow, and was beaten in his own apartment on November 11, 1975, so badly that he was hospitalized for two months. The assailants, who also robbed Kryuchkov of money, possessions, and some personal writings, were later identified by the police as three men who had escaped from a city psychiatric hospital that morning and admitted to the crime. The victim, however, denied that at least two of those held by the police were his attackers and, in a petition written by his lawyer, said the two men "did not take part in the assault and robbery, but for reasons unknown to Kryuchkov, confessed to the crime and thus shielded the real culprits."

It was also in the fall of 1975 that a young man at-

tacked Likhachov on a staircase landing in the Pushkin publishing house director's apartment building in Leningrad, breaking one of his ribs. The incident followed a KGB report to the publisher's party officials that certain Western circles were trying to convert Likhachov into a dissident and preceded an attempt on the night of May 1–2, 1976, to set fire to Likhachov's apartment. Although the door was smeared with plasticine and a can of gas had been left nearby, police said—as they had about the beating— that their investigation had been closed for lack of evidence. Aside from having served several years in Stalinist labor camps as a young man, Likhachov was one of the members of the Academy of Sciences who refused to sign the 1973 Academicians' attack on Sakharov.

In a lengthy interview on February 24, 1977, with a Newsweek *correspondent, Sakharov discussed at length the treatment of Soviet political prisoners and focused briefly on the growing interest in the 1975 Helsinki Accord as an instrument of human-rights leverage:*

Q: How many political prisoners are there now in the Soviet Union? How do you arrive at your conclusion?

A: I think that there are now about 2,000–5,000 political prisoners in the Soviet Union, but several Western sources and several Soviet citizens set the order of magnitude higher—at 20,000 people. I stick to the figure I cited. It is based on the population of those camps where I know political prisoners are held, adding, as a rough estimate, a certain percentage for prisoners located in other camps and psychiatric prisons. Unfortunately, in our country statistics are not published about such things. We do not know how many political prisoners there are, nor do we know how many prisoners there are in general, or the charges on which they have been convicted. Unofficial data, however, indicate that in our country we have 1–2 million prisoners —an extraordinarily high percentage of the general population in comparison to that of other developed countries.

Nevertheless, official propaganda claims that our crime rate is very low.

Q: What are medical conditions like for prisoners and in what ways are their human rights violated?

A: Camp and prison life is strictly regimented under the Corrective Labor Code. The Code certainly does not conform to international humanitarian standards and permits a whole range of human-rights violations to occur. I will cite a few examples. A person under arrest is completely isolated until the trial ends—he is allowed no meetings or correspondence even with his closest relatives; until the investigation is closed, he is not permitted to consult a lawyer—and the investigative process can take up to nine months or even a year. Once tried, and given the usual regimen allotted to the majority of political prisoners, he will have only two meetings with close family per year lasting up to four hours (often the authorities allot only two hours) and one meeting a year lasting a maximum of three days and nights (but often cut to a shorter period). The prisoners' correspondence is limited. In camps, prisoners are kept on starvation diets and only one 5-kilo food package per year can be sent to them, and that, only after half their sentence has been served. In strict forced-labor camps prisoners go almost unpaid—this is also regulated by the Code. But any and all rights that are, in fact, guaranteed by the Code may be denied a prisoner at the discretion of any representative of the prison administration. It is interesting to note that prisoners can qualify for amnesty only with the recommendation of the prison administration.

The Soviet Corrective Labor Code is a complete violation of rights; it fails to conform in any way to the maximum standards recommended by the UN. Prisoners who are believers (there are many of them) cannot have a Bible, the Gospels, the Koran, the Torah. They are forbidden to celebrate any religious rites. Medical services are primitive. Medicines are lacking, and sending medicines—even vitamins—to prisoners is prohibited. We know of only one decent hospital for prisoners—located in Leningrad—but the camp administration is not ashamed to say that political prisoners are never sent there.

It happens that at this moment we are trying to get Sergei Kovalev transferred there for an urgently needed operation.

Q: What about the rights of the families of these prisoners?

A: Theoretically the families should not suffer for the actions of their relatives, but in practice we know that this is not the case. Many family members have been demoted or are completely barred from employment. KGB agents frighten and terrorize the families. It is very hard when children are involved, especially those of school age. The path to a higher education is closed to them, but not in an official way—instead, in a humiliating and deceitful manner, these young people are given undeservedly low grades on examinations, etc. And even if a young person has already entered an institute, he will be given several failing marks on his year-end examinations and points will be deducted for supposed poor progress. This happened recently to the son of the priest Vasily Romanyuk.† The material situation of the families of political prisoners is usually difficult not only because the family is left without a father, but also because of the terrible expense of trips to the camp for meetings with the prisoner.

Q: What can the West do to help these prisoners and their families?

A: I think that showing concern for these families, either individually or as a group, is the best way to help. The assistance could take the form of money transfers, packages (which must be duty-paid in advance), letters to the families or to the prisoners themselves. Amnesty International does this kind of work. And this is very good. But one cannot forget that it is the duty of all honorable people the world over to fight for a general, worldwide political amnesty. Governments which do grant such an amnesty show their good-faith effort to solve the problems on which the future of humanity depends.

Q: What concrete human-rights proposals do you want the West to make at the Belgrade Meeting?

A: The Belgrade Meeting must, in my opinion, create conditions to guarantee that the humanitarian provisions of the Helsinki Final Act will be observed in practice, not just on paper.

Q: Is there a danger that public pressure exerted by the West could lead to the opposite result, to an increase in the number of arrests and to a still greater violation of human rights?

A: Weakness, or even the hint of weakness and vulnerability to blackmail, is inconsistent with the defense of human rights and can lead to tragic consequences. There can be only a positive effect from decisive and calmly increasing pressure by public and official Western opinion (right up to the top) in defense of general principles and specific people. Each instance of a human-rights violation must be turned into a political issue for the leaders of the countries that commit the violation.

Q: Is there a danger that by political arrests, exile, and intimidation the Soviet authorities can decrease the effectiveness of—even destroy—the so-called dissident movement? Do the arrests of Yuri Orlov,† Aleksandr Ginzburg,† and others indicate that the authorities have set out on this path? Will they succeed or will they always run up against other dissidents who will step forward to fight for human rights in the Soviet Union?

A: The arrests of Helsinki Watch Group members Ginzburg, Rudenko,† Tykhy,† and group leader Orlov apparently do signal a real attempt by Soviet authorities to strike a severe blow at the human-rights movement. However, this at the same time is taken as a call to action for world public opinion, to all the countries that were Helsinki signatories. I think that this point is understood by the West and that such an attempt by Soviet authorities will elicit strong opposition. In any case, without a doubt, as long as the reason for a human-rights movement exists in the USSR and Eastern Europe, it will continue.

Q: What influence did the Helsinki Accord have on the human-rights movement in the USSR? Did it foster a greater understanding and a much wider demand for the observance of these rights among the Soviet people?

A: The Helsinki Accord, along with the International Covenants on Human Rights, essentially made it possible to defend human rights more effectively and unarguably galvanized citizens in the USSR and Eastern Europe to press for their rights.

Q: Does Western pressure for human rights constitute interference in the internal affairs of the USSR? How can one refute such a charge?

A: It does not. The international character of the defense of human rights is established by the Universal Declaration of Human Rights, in the Covenants, and in the Helsinki Final Act. To assert that the defense of human rights is interference in the internal affairs of any country would mean to refute these documents' validity.

Q: What is the connection between international trust and the observance of fundamental human rights?

A: It is impossible to trust a government on an international level that violates the rights of its own citizens, rights that are guaranteed by international agreements that the government has signed and is obliged to respect. It is impossible to believe a government that violates human rights behind an iron, or if not iron, then still a sufficiently thick curtain. The world finds out about these violations because a human-rights movement exists. A closed society is in itself a violation of human rights and at the same time creates conditions that threaten international security.

X

The Helsinki Spirit

1977 was the year in which, by agreement, the thirty-five signatory states of the 1975 Helsinki Final Act of the Conference on Security and Cooperation in Europe were to meet in Belgrade to review their individual and collective progress in implementing the complex agreement on furthering politico-military security through economic, scientific, humanitarian, and cultural cooperation. The Final Act's provisions on human rights—binding NATO members, European neutrals, and Warsaw Pact nations to respect fundamental civil, political, religious, and social freedoms—had been seized on by ordinary citizens and active dissenters alike in the Eastern countries. Sakharov shared their hopes, and his wife joined the Soviet Helsinki Watch Group at its creation in May 1976. As this chapter indicates, however, the official Soviet response to citizen agitation for implementation of the Helsinki undertakings was, as often as not, to pursue and even intensify repression—imprisoning more and more of the Helsinki activists as the year passed and the Belgrade Meeting neared.

In a January 26, 1977, interview with a correspondent of the Italian daily Corriere della Sera, *Sakharov looked, with hope, at the rising tide of human-rights activity in Eastern Europe and, with alarm, at the pressure Soviet authorities were bringing against the flow:*

Q: In Communist countries, from the USSR to the —countries of Eastern Europe, the ranks of dissidents are growing. What do you think are the reasons behind this?

A: I am not sure that there has been a quantitative

growth, but without doubt we are now witnessing a new, qualitative change in the struggle for human rights. The main reasons for this development are the grave, unrelenting violations of all fundamental civil and political liberties, as well as many social and cultural rights, in the USSR and Eastern Europe. They continue despite the official proclamation of such goals and commitments as those given the force of law by the ratification of the International Covenant on Civil and Political Rights or set out in the humanitarian articles of the Helsinki Final Act. The nonviolent struggle for fundamental civil and political rights plays a special part in shaping the historical fate of our countries, international trust, and the future of all mankind. The fact that great numbers of people in our countries and in the West have come to understand this is another reason the human-rights movement has been able to develop and gain public support.

Q: How, in your opinion, do the dissidents in the USSR and Eastern Europe differ? What are the major distinctions between the societies which serve as the backdrop for the human rights struggle in the USSR and the countries of Eastern Europe?

A: In the USSR, which has lived through decades of historically unprecedented terror and political and civil degradation, wide sectors of workers, peasants, and the intelligentsia have become, for the most part, passive, intimidated, and dependent upon totalitarian rule. I do not mean to say that it has been easier for the people of Eastern Europe. But nevertheless, the circumstances in these countries differ from the Soviet situation. The countries of Eastern Europe have always been closer to the West with its humanitarian and democratic traditions of inherent respect for individual rights. In certain of these countries, especially Poland, the church traditionally has exerted a great and beneficial influence, which it has managed to preserve under very difficult conditions. Of no small importance, finally, is the fact that the countries of Eastern Europe are held in a relationship of intolerable dependence with the USSR. The dissidents' logical demand to be freed from this dependence has found echoes throughout the population, thus expanding the base of the human-rights movement in these countries.

Nevertheless, I do think that the similarities and common aims in the human-rights movements in the USSR and the countries of Eastern Europe are much more significant in the wider historical perspective than all the differences I have noted here.

All of us in the USSR feel great admiration for the new escalation of activity on the part of our East European friends—the organizers of Charter '77 in Czechoslovakia, the Workers' Defense Committee in Poland, and others. We will never forget the role of the Prague Spring of 1968 in the formation of the human-rights movement in the USSR.

Q: Do you think that any links between Soviet and East European dissidents will form in the future?

A: One of the fundamental features of totalitarian societies is that information exchange is blocked both within a country and across its borders. Only monumental efforts (and sometimes even sacrifice) have made it possible to maintain as much contact with Western countries as there is now; any slackening in the attention this problem receives at any given moment threatens the gains already achieved. Other dissidents and I cannot pick up a telephone and call our friends in Eastern Europe; nor can we write them letters. Of course, we would all like to have free personal contact, or even better, the opportunity to issue joint statements, as well as less formal means of coordinating our efforts. Perhaps international support will someday provide us with such opportunities—which would not be important only for our countries. But nevertheless, it is my feeling now that even at a distance we have a definite, albeit incomplete, understanding of one another, a feeling of touching elbows.

Q: How do you assess Charter '77 and the official Soviet reaction to it?

A: I see Charter '77 as a historic document representing an important new step in the struggle for human rights not only in Czechoslovakia but in all Communist countries. It is of special relevance that Charter '77 bases itself on the most important international documents—the Universal Declaration of Human Rights; the International Covenant, which has the force of law; and the Helsinki Final Act— and illustrates the discrepancies between the real situation and the principles these documents promote. The very spirit of Charter '77, its restrained pathos and force, evoke great sympathy in me. The fact that this document was signed by three hundred° citizens of the CSSR and, without doubt, supported by many others throughout the country, was the factor which provoked the authorities' rage and made them organize false spectacles of public censure.

The Soviet press reaction to Charter '77 is very significant. It poses a threat not only to Czechoslovakian, but to Soviet dissidents. As usual, of course, Charter '77 itself was never published or even quoted, a fact which simply shows how incapable official propaganda is of waging an honest, open struggle of ideas on any sort of equal ground.

Q: Do you think that this document could be accepted by Soviet dissidents?

A: I think it could. The whole spirit of the document is undoubtedly close to Soviet dissidents. As for me, if Charter '77 were to grant citizens of other countries the right to sign it, I would request that this statement be considered my signature, and that of my wife, Elena Bonner.

Q: What type of aid can dissidents in the USSR and Eastern Europe expect from Western Communist parties?

A: The dissident movement, or, to be exact, the human-rights movement in our countries, is not political in nature. Its participants hold divergent views of the world. We feel that this movement is of significance not only for the future of our countries, but for all of mankind. We rely on the support of all honest, humane, and farsighted people throughout the world, regardless of their political platform.

We have a special need for open discussion, for widespread and objective publicity on the real facts about our countries, facts undistorted by official propaganda. If the Communist press were to report such facts—in particular,

° Over nine hundred in mid-1978.—Ed.

to speak in defense of political prisoners and freedom of conscience, to foster information exchange, and uphold the free flow of people—it would make an important contribution to the human-rights movement.

Dissidents usually end up being fired from work. This is why they and their families, as well as the families of political prisoners, need material support.

I feel that the Communist parties which proclaim the concept of pluralistic Communism with a human face should in fact dissociate themselves even more decisively from the government and party policies of totalitarian countries, and should be insisting on the actual practice of fundamental civil and political rights.

Q: Do you think that the pressure on dissidents has intensified recently?

A: I believe it has. One reason is the escalation of the human-rights struggle, which the authorities cannot deal with on the field of honest discussion. Another reason: the imminence of the Belgrade Meeting. To compromise and to crush the dissidents during this period is a tempting goal for the organs of repression. Searches, interrogations, arrests, provocations, threats of physical force, and possibly even direct acts of secret terror—all of these have been set in motion. The still-uninvestigated murder of the poet-translator Konstantin Bogatyrev,† a former prisoner in Stalinist camps, is one of many examples.

It seems that the authorities want to tear apart the Helsinki Watch Groups in the USSR (Moscow, Kiev, Vilnius) and have conducted a series of searches to advance this aim. The planting of money and pornographic publications to compromise group participants has been one distinctive feature of these searches.

After the explosion in the Moscow subway, the danger that this event might be used to intensify repressions arose, an event that possibly was the handiwork of the KGB. The bloody past of the secret police supports such fears, as does Victor Louis' article. The purpose of my article° was to

° See Chapter V. —Ed.

inform world public opinion of these threatening possibilities, and to issue a warning against such a course. When this article led to my being summoned to the Procurator's Office of the USSR, I was pressed to write a retraction and given an official warning that I would be held criminally responsible if I did not stop my public activity. Such warnings frequently foreshadow arrest. Nevertheless, Mafia-type tactics are a greater danger to my family and myself.

The obstruction of international ties (through the mails and by telephone) has served as an official tactic used to block publicity—the dissidents' solitary weapon. The Italian telephone agency can confirm that even personal telephone calls are impossible because of KGB operators, as shown by attempts my wife and I made to put through a call to learn of the state of health of Dr. Nina Harkevich, a close friend in Florence.

Earlier, in the October 30, 1976, interview with an American correspondent, Sakharov spoke of Soviet gestures toward Helsinki compliance against the background of stubborn immovability:

Q: The Soviet government has often stated that it would fulfill all the commitments made in the Helsinki Final Act. Do you feel that it is doing so?

A: The concept of the free flow of information and of people (trips abroad as well as emigration) is a key element of the Final Act. The document's historical importance lies in the unbreakable link it establishes between these provisions and international security. Yet the Soviet Union has hardly made any change in its practices in the sphere of information flow and the movement of peoples. The isolated concessions which have been made, mostly on emigration and travel, are of some significance, but they do not yet amount to fundamental change in the overall picture.

Soviet citizens still have no way to obtain a great deal of Western information on political, historical, social, economic, religious, and cultural issues. Decisions on emigration and travel abroad still are very difficult to obtain and are subject to terrible arbitrariness from which there is no appeal. Consequently, tens of thousands still suffer great personal tragedies.

Even something as simple and natural, from a Western perspective, as a meeting between mother and daughter can be forbidden—sometimes for years at a stretch. I can cite the case of Dr. Vera Livchak, about whom I have spoken and written more than once.

Dr. Livchak, a physician who was seventy-two years old in 1977, was widowed in 1962; her daughter emigrated with her husband to Israel in 1971, but Dr. Livchak's requests to make a visit either to Israel or to Austria—just to see her daughter—or to obtain permission for the daughter to return as a tourist to Moscow have all been refused.

In a letter referring to Brezhnev's signature of the Final Act, Dr. Livchak wrote:

"I have received the following oral responses (OVIR does not respond in writing). With respect to Israel: We do not have diplomatic relations with Israel. And Austria: Your daughter lives in Israel. There are no reasons for you to meet in Austria. And with regard to her visiting me in Moscow: The situation is not appropriate.

"Rather than grant me permission to visit my daughter, the authorities proposed that I leave Russia, renounce my Soviet citizenship, and leave for permanent residence in Israel. That is to say, they proposed I do all that people wishing to leave Russia must do, all the things authorities then label high treason.

"I am a Russian. I was employed without interruption from 1919 through February 1977. From 1926 on, I worked as a doctor. In 1954, I was awarded an order for my work. I have elderly and ailing brothers and sisters here, my husband's relatives and friends. The dear graves of my husband and mother are here. Why, for what crimes, must I in my old age break off my life and leave all of this? I feel that it is my human right to be able to see my only daughter without rupturing my life."

Finally despairing of a favorable reply, Dr. Livchak dropped her fight for a temporary travel permit and emigrated from the USSR in August 1978.

On November 20, 1976, Sakharov sent a message of solidarity to the Polish intellectuals who had formed a Workers' Defense Committee to protest the maltreatment of workers whose June strike to protest high food prices had succeeded in getting costs rolled back:

I support the initiative of the representatives of the Polish intelligentsia, headed by Jerzy Andrzejewski, who created the Workers' Defense Committee to protect workers from reprisals inflicted by the authorities.

In our country, as in Poland, there are many problems which touch the widest strata of the population, including workers. Undoubtedly, the struggle for workers' rights constitutes an important part of the democratic movement for human rights. In the USSR we clearly understand this, although at the present time I am unaware of any concrete actions which could rank with the activity of the Polish Workers' Defense Committee in scope and effectiveness.

We know the importance of nonconformity and solidarity under totalitarian conditions, and we also know how difficult they are to maintain. I admire the boldness of our friends in Poland who, in dealing with these real and immediate problems, are expressing the solidarity of intellectuals and workers.

I hope that in time ways will be found for effective cooperation in the struggle for human rights in Poland, the USSR, and the other countries of Eastern Europe.

On November 29, "reprisals" came closer to home, when Soviet authorities took steps to block an international gathering organized by "refuseniks" in Moscow to explore the state of Jewish culture in the USSR. The meeting's organizers were subjected to a variety of harassments —even though their project met the general standard for

international cultural cooperation activities set in the Hel-
sinki Accord—and Sakharov quickly gave them his backing:

Soviet officials are attempting to break off a symposium
which holds a significance not only for Jewish culture, but
for all the other national cultures of our country as well.
An ethnic-cultural undertaking such as this could serve as
an important precedent following decades of stagnation in
the free development of national cultures.

I appeal to the international community to support
this symposium.

As planned, the symposium would have featured
seventy-seven papers on six different topics (covering Jew-
ish culture in Israel and the West, as well as in the USSR),
with eighteen papers assigned to foreign scholars. After
nine members of the organizing committee were subjected
to house searches in Moscow on November 23–24, a TASS
statement appeared justifying the searches because "the
materials seized bear witness to the ties with Zionist cen-
ters and to the aim of inciting national discord in the
Soviet Union." Within a few days, moreover, articles on
the successful development of Jewish culture in the USSR
began to appear for the first time in many years in the
official Soviet press. Deputy Culture Minister Vladimir
Popov, however, received the symposium's organizers to
tell them that only "registered civic organizations" could
engage in cultural undertakings and that their plans would
"contradict the existing order." Although the symposium
was to begin December 21—and did open that day for a
one-day, seven-paper session attended by some fifty people,
including Sakharov—all the Moscow organizers were put
under three-day house arrest that morning, a reported
twenty participants from other Soviet cities were detained
by police en route to the capital, and of the thirty foreign-
ers invited to take part, not one was able to obtain a visa.

In early February came the first arrests of Helsinki
Watchers—Ukrainian activists Mykola Rudenko† and Olek-

sei Tykhy† and Muscovite Aleksandr Ginzburg,† a leading light of Soviet dissent since the early 1960s. Sakharov joined the mathematician Igor Shafarevich—a friend of Solzhenitsyn and a fellow member of the Moscow Human Rights Committee—in an appeal that day for Ginzburg:

Aleksandr Ginzburg, representative of the Solzhenitsyn Fund for assistance to political prisoners and member of the Helsinki Watch Group, has been arrested. For five years he has been subjected to continuous harassment: he has been denied the right to live with his family, searched, detained, and subjected to an outpouring of repulsive filthy slander in the pages of Soviet newspapers. Now he is in prison again. This is his third arrest. If he is sentenced, he will get the striped uniform of an especially dangerous recidivist, a "special regimen" camp, reduced food rations, one letter per month, one personal visit per year, a one-kilogram parcel per year, and one food package per year —beginning only after half the term has been served.

Aleksandr Ginzburg has just been discharged from the hospital under instructions to go to a tuberculosis clinic for examinations and cure. The diagnosis: pneumonia compounded by tubercular infection. After seven years in camps, he suffers from grave stomach and intestinal ulcers. One need not be a doctor to understand that even a short-term imprisonment could be fatal for him.

Seized at night on the street, Ginzburg was driven to Kaluga, where it would be easier to hold an illegal trial far from friends and foreign correspondents.

At the Moscow KGB inquiry desk, Ginzburg's wife was told that he had been accused under several articles of the Criminal Code; however, the specific articles were not cited. In a TASS announcement, references are made to speculation in icons, anti-Soviet activity, ties to an "anti-Soviet organization," foreign currency. An article published in *Literaturnaya Gazeta* on the eve of Ginzburg's arrest has demonstrated that the false witnesses are now ready.

There is every reason to fear that the arrest of Aleksandr Ginzburg is a link in the chain of repressions in preparation for the Belgrade Meeting. How far this wave continues, and where it will end this time, depends on the reaction of Soviet and world public opinion.

We appeal to all those who agree that the defense of human rights is essential for the preservation of peace on earth.

Our joint obligation is the defense of Aleksandr Ginzburg.

The editor has arranged the following text, possibly inaccurate in places, of TASS's "Statement for Abroad":

Ginzburg was arrested with the approval of the Procurator of the town of Kaluga, for activities which are at variance with the law. Ginzburg, without permanent employment, a parasite, began his career as a profiteer and dealer in icons.

In 1961 he was sentenced to two years for fraud, and in 1968[?] to five years for anti-Soviet activity. At that time his involvement with the pro-Fascist émigré organization NTS had already been disclosed, an organization which, as is well known, is secretly engaged in work for the West.

After his release he continued actively to engage in anti-Soviet activities, the specific nature of which, it is hoped, will be revealed in the course of the present investigation. As has already been reported, a search was conducted of Ginzburg's apartment, which resulted in the discovery of materials which testify to his unquestionable involvement with NTS, of anti-Soviet brochures, Zionist lampoons, and large quantities of Soviet and foreign currency.

Aleksandr Ginzburg was actively pursued by the civilian police, who accused him of "violation of registration regulations." For example, as a result of these requirements he was forced, every three days, to leave his family, who live in Moscow, and return to Tarusa, where he was registered. A statement issued by Sakharov, referring to one incident during those many months of harassment by the civilian police, is given here:

To the Barbinskoye section of the civilian police, from A. D. Sakharov

I herewith register my protest against the doubly illegal (June 2 and 7) and groundless detention of A. I. Ginzburg, a man under contractual employment to myself, in my summer house in the settlement of Zhukov, for the fabricated reason that he is residing in Zhukov without the proper registration. For this detention, which was conducted in my absence and in violation of my rights as owner of the summer house, a report was drawn up and a fine imposed on Ginzburg. On June 7 representatives of the civilian police, without any warrant, forcefully entrenched themselves in my summer house, hampering the movement of my family, and in spite of my demand over the phone that Ginzburg be left alone and that they withdraw from my home, they forcefully removed Ginzburg.

I declare that A. Ginzburg did not even once come to my house for more than a few hours at a time, that not once did he spend the night, so that any violation of registration requirements is out of the question. I venture that the men who have established this surveillance over myself and my summer house are in fact with the KGB—no one knows this better than I. What is even more astonishing is that, on June 7, when the report was drawn up at the Barbinskoye section of the civilian police, perjurers were brought in who corroborated the statement concerning a violation of registration requirements which never actually took place. These people don't live in Zhukov and have never seen Ginzburg. On June 7 Ginzburg left for the summer house by train at 10:45 from Kursk station, so perhaps my wife's and my own witnesses' statements should serve as corroboration.

I demand that the report of the Barbinskoye section of the civilian police, which supports deliberately false charges, be invalidated.

I claim that these actions are a form of persecution, not only of Ginzburg, but of myself as well.

> A. D. Sakharov
> three-time Socialist Hero of Labor
> June 7, 1976

Yuri Orlov,† founder of the Helsinki Watch, was arrested February 10, and on March 15—after a former room-

mate and fellow "refusednik" denounced him and other Jews as being in the service of the CIA—Anatoly Shcharansky† was jailed. Sakharov responded with an appeal on March 19 to "world public opinion," the U.S. Congress, and the Final Act signatory governments:

Anatoly Shcharansky was arrested on March 15. We all read the slanderous article in *Izvestia* which evoked recollections of the worst of the Stalinist "witch hunts." The article absurdly charges Shcharansky and other Jewish activists with espionage. Along with these individuals, American citizens also stand openly and falsely accused. The truth, nevertheless, is that Shcharansky, who applied to emigrate to Israel three years ago and received a groundless refusal, led such an open life that there can be no question of any sort of secret activity. He openly protested the violation of the right to emigrate and other human rights. He openly joined the Helsinki Watch Group and openly met with foreign correspondents and guests from abroad. Never, neither in the past as a student nor at the present time, has he had any contacts with state secrets. He has not committed any state crimes. I am convinced that it was just because of his boldness and openness, his consistently honest and humane attitude, that the authorities chose him as their next victim.

In seeking to reverse the rising tide of interest in the human-rights problem throughout the world over the last few months, the authorities have chosen a foolish course, but their success or failure will be of great and lasting significance for the whole world.

Shcharansky's arrest, following the arrests of other Helsinki Watch Group members, is an act of defiance the Soviet authorities have added to their game of provocation before the Belgrade Meeting. It amounts to an attempt to blackmail the new U.S. administration before the visit of Secretary of State Vance, an attempt to force the Administration to renounce its worldwide human-rights policy and to consolidate an official license for the Soviets to wreak lawlessness.

It is crucial for humanity to defend Shcharansky, Ginz-

burg, Orlov, Rudenko, and Tykhy, for their defense is also
the defense of the spirit of détente, international trust, and
peace.

*Inexorably, however, fresh arrests followed, and on
April 13, Sakharov appealed again for international help
from public opinion and the Helsinki signatories' leaders:*

A new wave of political repression is swelling in the
USSR. The arrests of Zviad Gamsakhurdia† and Merab
Kostava† in Georgia on April 7 followed on the heels of
the arrests of members of the Helsinki Watch Groups in
Moscow and the Ukraine in February and March. Two
more honest and courageous men have fallen into the
hands of the cruel and contemptuous investigative apparatus. What can they be accused off? Anything: foreign
currency dealings, rape, hooliganism, terrorism, anything
at all. But they were arrested for aspiring toward truth
and free and open discussion, and for striving to preserve
the national culture of their ancient and beautiful country,
its monuments, language, and authentic art. Each Georgian,
and each person in our country, cannot help but be proud
of such fellow countrymen. We are indignant over this
new demonstration of lawlessness. The arrests of Gamsakhurdia and Kostava are yet another step the authorities
have taken in their attempts to stifle the voice of dissenters
so that they can arrive at the Belgrade Meeting with their
country kept in dead silence.

I appeal once again to the public and the leadership
of the USSR, Europe, and the U.S.A., and world public
opinion, to come out in defense of the arrested Helsinki
Watch Group members Gamsakhurdia, Kostava, Ginzburg,
Orlov, Rudenko, Tykhy, and Shcharansky.

*On June 11, Sakharov, Shafarevich, Valentin Turchin,
Naum Meiman, and Yuri Goldfarb sent a joint appeal to
their colleagues meeting in the 1977 Protvino Conference
on Accelerators to show scientific solidarity in aid of an-*

other physicist, Yuri Orlov, the imprisoned founder of the Helsinki Watch Groups:

Yuri Orlov, a physicist of world repute, a major specialist in the field of accelerators, Corresponding Member of the Armenian Academy of Sciences, was arrested in February of this year and is now in Lefortovo Prison.

He was arrested for his active struggle for human rights in our country and for his role as founder and leader of the Helsinki Watch Groups.

The activity of the groups has been and continues to be open and legal, but Orlov nevertheless stands charged with the absurd "dissemination of slanderous inventions," and the threat of a three-year sentence looms over him.

Other group members are under arrest as well—Aleksandr Ginzburg and Anatoly Shcharansky in Moscow; Mykola Rudenko, Oleksei Tykhy, Mykola Matusevych,† and Myroslav Marynovych† in Kiev; Zviad Gamsakhurdia and Merab Kostava in Tbilisi. Two have already been tried —writer and war invalid Mykola Rudenko, and Oleksei Tykhy, a teacher. Their trial was effectively a closed one, and their right to defense was also flagrantly violated. They were sentenced: Tykhy to ten years' imprisonment and five years' exile; Rudenko to seven years' imprisonment and five of exile. Group member Malva Landa,† a geologist, has already begun serving her two years in exile.

We appeal to the participants of this conference, to the colleagues of Yuri Orlov, with a call that you demand the Soviet authorities' immediate release of Orlov and a public examination in the press of the charges brought against him.

We call upon you to demand that the leaders of Soviet science express their opinion on the Orlov case.

We would also value your concern for the fates of the other repressed group members.

Presumably to avoid embarrassment at the Belgrade Meeting, Soviet authorities waited until the sessions ended in March 1978 to resume the trials of the arrested Helsinki

*Watchers. Marynovych and Matusevych were first—March
29—to receive "anti-Soviet agitation" sentences of seven
years in prison camp and five in exile, the same sentence
imposed on Yuri Orlov on May 18 in Moscow, after the
charge against him was raised from Article 190.1 to Article
70. In the same week, but in Tbilisi, Gamsakhurdia and
Kostava were sentenced to three years in camp and two
of exile, following Soviet press reports that Gamsakhurdia,
at least, had admitted his guilt in court. While the Orlov
trial was under way, Vladimir Slepak and his wife hung a
banner stating their demand to emigrate to Israel from the
balcony of their Moscow apartment and were arrested for
"malicious hooliganism." On June 21, 1978, Slepak and another "refusednik" activist, Ida Nudel, who had taken part
in a demonstration protesting the Slepaks' arrest, were both
sentenced in separate Moscow trials to five years in exile;
Mrs. Slepak's trial was first postponed because of her illness—a bleeding ulcer; but she was later given a suspended
sentence of exile. In July Viktoras Petkus,† Ginzburg, and
Shcharansky were all tried, convicted and sentenced to
ten-year, eight-year, and thirteen-year terms, respectively.
Thus, of fifty-eight members of the Soviet Helsinki Watch
and its affiliates, fourteen have been sentenced to long
prison-camp terms, two have been exiled, and two—who
were traveling in the West—have been stripped of their
Soviet citizenship.*

*As the next two appeals show, Sakharov attached a
special importance to the Helsinki pledges of fair treatment for families seeking to be reunited. On July 23, 1977,
he reacted angrily to reports that one such family had
been beaten:*

Mr. and Mrs. Chudnovsky were assaulted on the street
near their home in Kiev last evening. One assailant beat
the two old, sick people while two others looked on. The
wife, who had recently suffered from insulin shock, received a concussion and a dislocated shoulder; her hus-

band is also in critical condition. The militia arrived only four and a half hours later.

The incident occurred after the Chudnovskys' fate had attracted attention both in the USSR and abroad. There are reasons to believe that the assault was planned and sanctioned as an intimidation.

In January of this year, the Chudnovskys and their two sons applied to emigrate to Israel. In April, authorities denied them permission without indicating any reasons for the denial. For the Chudnovsky family, emigration is the only hope for more effective treatment for their younger son, Grigory, who has been bedridden since childhood with myasthenia gravis.

Grigory is a talented mathematician, and I hope that his fate in particular will attract the attention of mathematicians around the world. Along with another author, and independently, Grigory solved Hilbert's extremely difficult tenth problem. He has also produced many original and significant results in the theory of differential equations, algebraic topology, and the theory of numbers.

Grigory's parents are retired scientific workers. David, his older brother, is also a mathematician, candidate for a postdoctoral degree in physical and mathematical sciences, co-author of some of Grigory's works, and also an invalid who has dedicated his whole life selflessly to assisting his younger brother.

I request that all wire services, newspapers, and radio stations promote the dissemination of this information. I call on world public opinion, all mathematicians, all government and public organizations who have undertaken the defense of human rights, to fight the pogromists and support the Chudnovsky family and their right immediately to emigrate.

The Chudnovskys were allowed to emigrate the following month, but Naum Meiman and Yuri Goldfarb, who had joined Sakharov in the Orlov appeal, were (and still are) barred from leaving when Sakharov wrote the following open letter on their behalf to Dr. George Rathjens and

Dr. Jeremy Stone, respectively chairman and director of the Federation of American Scientists, on September 9, 1977:

I am very anxious for the fate of two scientists, mathematician Naum Meiman and physicist Yuri Goldfarb, who are not being allowed to emigrate from the USSR. Authorities issuing refusals say that Meiman and Goldfarb had access to secret information. I am well acquainted with the work of Meiman and Goldfarb, with their level of knowledge concerning secret issues, and I feel it is my duty and responsibility to state that there are no grounds to the authorities' claims.

Until 1954, Naum Meiman participated in computer projects at the Institute of Physical Problems in Moscow, which were commissioned by the Nuclear Weapons Systems Research Center. Yuri Goldfarb, until 1956, took part in similar projects at the Physics Institute of the Lebedev Academy of Sciences of the USSR in Moscow. Persons working outside the Nuclear Weapons Systems Research Center were as a rule not apprised of concrete facts and the actual parameters and characteristics of these systems. This applied especially to persons not in charge of a given project. Therefore, information Meiman and Goldfarb could divulge could never have been of any significance. And now, more than twenty years after their work on secret projects, Goldfarb and Meiman undoubtedly have no classified information at their disposal.

All these years they have worked productively in the abstract fields of theoretical physics and mathematics. Their desire to emigrate is based on very weighty considerations. Many years of visa denials have placed them in an extremely difficult situation.

I appeal to the Federation of American Scientists to support the right of Goldfarb and Meiman to emigrate.

At the end of September, Sakharov summed up his views on the Helsinki process in a forceful "Appeal to the Parliaments of All Helsinki-Signatory States." Written on the eve of the October 4 opening of the Belgrade Meeting, it was delivered in Moscow to the embassies of Aus-

*tria, France, the Federal Republic of Germany, Great
Britain, Italy, the Netherlands, and Norway. It was also
made available to* The New York Times, *which printed an
edited and abridged version of it on the Op-Ed page on
October 4. The full text follows:*

Two years ago, the Final Act of the Helsinki Conference on Security and Cooperation in Europe was signed.
Its historical significance was the proclamation of an inseparable bond between international security and an open
society—that is, the freedom of conscience.

Is the West prepared to defend these noble and vitally
important principles? Or will it gradually, in silence, ac-
quiesce in the interpretation of the principles of Helsinki,
and of détente as a whole, that the leaders of the Soviet
Union and of Eastern Europe are trying to impose?

That the principles of Helsinki would have to be defended was clear from the very beginning. The Soviet and
East European representatives have always tried to neu-
tralize the humanitarian sections of the Helsinki Accord by
emphasizing the principle of noninterference in the internal affairs of other countries. But the fact is that these
allusions are out of place, and contradict the United Nations Charter, the Covenant on Civil and Political Rights,
the Universal Declaration of Human Rights, and the Final
Act itself, where violations of human rights, accepted international standards of civil rights, and the openness of
society are concerned.

At the same time, the Soviet Union and other socialist
countries think it quite permissible to conduct their own
impudent campaign against real and imagined violations of
human rights in the West.

Such a one-sided understanding of détente is not limited to words (and I am only talking about human rights).
Every person serving a term in the hell of the present-day
Gulag for his beliefs, or open profession of them—every victim of psychiatric repression for political reasons, every
person refused permission to emigrate or travel abroad—
represents a direct violation of the Helsinki Accord.

I am referring to persecution for religious activity; to

the refusal to allow emigration of Pentecostals and Baptists, many Germans and Jews, people of other nationalities; to the repressions directed against Kovalev, Gluzman,† Vins,† Romanyuk,† Soldatov,† Ogurtsov,† Semyonova,† Sergienko,† Kiirend,† Osipov,† Superfin,† Gajauskas,† Chornovil,† Ruban, and hundreds of others for their lawful, humanitarian activities; to the suffering imposed on persons for attempts to flee the country; and especially to the alarming fact of repressions against those who gather and publish materials on the violations of the humanitarian provisions of the Helsinki Accords, organize groups monitoring their fulfillment, and belong to such groups.

The monstrous cruelty of the sentences imposed this year on the Ukrainians Mykola Rudenko and Oleksei Tykhy, out of sight of the public and in violation of their rights to a legal defense; the arrests of Yuri Orlov, Aleksandr Ginzburg, Anatoly Shcharansky, Myroslav Marynovych, Mykola Matusevych, Zviad Gamsakhurdia, Merab Kostava, Felix Serebrov,† and Viktoras Petkus; and the internal exile of Malva Landa (all members of Helsinki Watch Groups in the USSR) are not simply routine violations of the right of freedom of conscience, but a defiant act by the Soviet authorities—a test of the West's resolve to insist on the fulfillment of the principles of Helsinki.

To ignore this challenge would be a faint-hearted capitulation to blackmail. It is hardly necessary to add that this would probably have further negative consequences in all aspects of East-West relations without exception, including the fundamental issues of international security.

I believe Western parliaments should insist that their delegations to the meeting opening in Belgrade carry the sort of official instructions which would preclude any such surrender. It is essential to insist on the immediate release of those convicted or arrested for the expression of criticism, on the facilitation of emigration and foreign travel, and on the free sale of books, newspapers, and magazines published abroad. These are prerequisites for the successful conduct and conclusion of the Belgrade Meeting.

I am appealing especially to the Congress of the United States. President Carter, supported by the great power and influence of his country and guided by the express will and traditions of a freedom-loving people, proclaimed that the defense of human rights throughout the world is the moral foundation of United States policy. Now it is essential to give these principles energetic support.

We are living through a period of history in which decisive support of the principles of freedom of conscience, an open society, and the rights of man is an absolute necessity. The alternative is surrender to totalitarianism, the loss of all precious freedom, and political, economic, and moral degradation.

The West, its political and moral leaders, its free and decent peoples, must not allow this.

Publication of this appeal evoked from the Soviet press a new wave of vituperation for foreign consumption. Two Novosti press articles written for release abroad on October 19 and 26, respectively, harked back to the Gusev warning of January, one declaring ominously that "the Soviet public cannot remain indifferent to Sakharov's antipatriotic and antisocial activities which frequently contradict Soviet law." In November, the magazine Novoye Vremya *(New Times), also for circulation outside the USSR, added new charges: "pathological individualism" and "unhealthy arrogance."*

But the greatest harm, in Sakharov's eyes, came from distortions of his appeal by The New York Times. *He saw errors of translation and abridgements of the appeal as evidence of the "cavalier" journalistic approach to his work which, in another context, he had said "nearly unhinged" him. In a letter written October 10—and printed by the* Times *in full on February 4, 1978—he appealed to the editors of the* Times *and the* International Herald Tribune, *as well as to the Soviet division of the Voice of America, to correct the record. At the end of that letter, he voiced again a plea for full, undistorted treatment of documents of dissent in the Western press:*

On September 27, 1977, I handed over to a correspondent of your paper the text of my Appeal to the Parliaments of all countries signatory to the Helsinki Final Act for publication on the opening day of the Belgrade Meeting. I was pleased that publication did occur, regarding the event as the fulfillment of my duty and yours toward the defense of human rights. Naturally, such a text should be published in a complete and accurate translation from the original. Unfortunately, as it was printed in *The New York Times* and the *Herald Tribune* and broadcast by the Voice of America to the USSR, there were significant changes made from the original, done without the consent of the author of the Appeal. Even publication of this sort had a definitely positive significance, but the meaning was markedly weakened. I request that this letter, containing the necessary corrections of the text, be published in both papers and broadcast by radio.

1. Restore my heading. [In *The New York Times* the title was: "By Sakharov and About Him." —Ed.] I did not write a newspaper article but an Appeal to Parliaments, directed to specific addressees and requiring definite responses. It is appropriate to recall that I personally handed over the text of the Appeal in the embassies of eight Helsinki signatories. It was an unusual act in our circumstances.

2. My text read: "I am appealing especially to the Congress of the United States. President Carter, supported by the great power and influence of his country and guided by the express will and traditions of a freedom-loving people, proclaimed that the defense of human rights throughout the world is the moral foundation of United States policy. *Now it is essential to give these principles energetic support.*" In the newspaper article ascribed to me, the text appeared: "I particularly appeal to the United States Congress and President Carter, supported by the enormous power and influence of his country, drawing on the clearly expressed will and tradition of a free people, to declare the defense of human rights in the whole world to be a fundamental moral policy of the United States." Thus the call to action was replaced with a call for yet another declaration. I consider such treatment of my text to have been completely cavalier and a distortion of its political content.

3. Restore my original text (with the slight correction of the underlined words): "I am referring to persecution for religious activity; to the refusal to allow emigration of Pentecostals and Baptists, many Germans and Jews, people of other nationalities; to the repressions directed against Kovalev, Gluzman, Vins, Romanyuk, Soldatov, Ogurtsov, Semyonova, Sergienko, Kiirend, Osipov, Superfin, *Gajauskas, Chornovil,* Ruban, and hundreds of others for their lawful, humanitarian activities; to the suffering imposed on persons for attempts to flee the country; and *especially to the alarming fact* of repressions against those who *gather and publish* materials on the violations of the humanitarian provisions of the Helsinki Accords. . . . The monstrous cruelty of the sentences imposed this year on Rudenko and Tykhy, the arrests of Orlov, Ginzburg, Shcharansky, Marynovych, Matusevych, Gamsakhurdia, Kostava, Petkus, Serebrov, and the internal exile of Malva Landa are not simply routine violations of the right of freedom of conscience, but a defiant act by the Soviet authorities—a test of the West's resolve to insist on the fulfillment of the principles of Helsinki."

The newspaper dropped the names of all but five members of the Helsinki Watch Groups, distorting the overall sense of the paragraph. The struggle and suffering of Kovalev and the others whom I mentioned merit more respectful treatment. We here are convinced that mention in the press and on the radio of specific individuals is very important; it has a real, practical impact. Materials about those I mentioned and other dissenters are available to any Western editor. (They can be found, for example, at the Khronika Press in New York.) It is very easy to comment on my text itself, if so desired. Now, during the Belgrade Meeting, political prisoners in the USSR are conducting hunger strikes, fighting not for themselves, but for the principles which should be dear to all freedom-loving people. Let us be worthy of them!

I attach major significance to the correction of the omissions and distortions. Similar episodes occur far too often with publications by me and other dissenters. We are waging a hard fight here, accompanied by heavy sacrifices, for public awareness. Thus it is intolerable when distortions of our voices, projected with great difficulty to the West, deny us even partially the fruits of our struggle.

Sakharov's voice, however, was being heard in the West and heeded. He and Anatoly Shcharansky were named co-winners of the Joseph Prize for Human Rights, given by the Anti-Defamation League of B'nai B'rith. Accepting the prize at a Washington dinner in November addressed by Vice-President Walter Mondale, Stanford University physicist Sidney Drell read a note of thanks Sakharov had written in Moscow on November 4:

I am very grateful for this honor. It is of significance to me that the League has presented me with this award along with Anatoly Shcharansky, who is now threatened with a harsh sentence on a false and absurd charge.

All dissenters in our country and in Eastern Europe have always been victims of defamation, be they free or behind prison doors or barbed wire. The vast majority of dissenters in the USSR reject force on principle and employ the true free word as their only weapon. In response, the authorities, retaining the crudest forms of force and tyranny, widely use slander against them, on the pages of the monolithic press, at meetings, in political instructions, and in courtrooms. The task of neutralizing this weapon is a noble one for the defense of human rights around the world. I hope that the League's activity promotes and will continue to promote this task.

I express my gratitude to you once again.

An even larger American organization, the American Federation of Labor–Congress of Industrial Organizations, honored Sakharov by inviting him to address its 1977 convention in Los Angeles. Unable to attend, he wrote the following speech on November 28 to be read at the gathering:

The opportunity to speak here is a great honor for me. I want to express my gratitude to you and to your chairman, Mr. Meany.

We in the USSR know of the influence on domestic and international affairs which the AFL–CIO has in your country. We have great respect for your evaluation of such vital matters as the proper tasks of foreign policy, of economic, scientific-technological, and cultural ties, and of aid to developing countries. We also greatly respect your responsible understanding of the tasks of U.S. economic prosperity and national security—on which depends the future of not only the American people—as well as your approach toward the defense of human rights. This role of your organization, which represents the interests of the broadest strata of working people, is one of the manifestations of the pluralistic nature of American society which is surprising to us: surprising because these manifestations are in striking contrast to what we see in our own country. In this pluralism, in democracy, lies the enormous, real power of your society, the profound source of its successes. It is, of course, true that our single-party, single-ideology, closed, caste society is in many ways different from your society. And yet, not so different that we cannot understand your problems, and you ours; not so different that we cannot try to work out some sort of common course of conduct.

It is said that the character of the American people, its active and practical goodwill and feeling of its own worth, is expressed in the question—which has become a national tradition—"Can I help you?" It seems to me that in inviting me to this meeting, you are in effect also asking me this question. I will try to answer it, for we are dealing here not simply with help to us, but above all with the defense of universal human values, the universal future of mankind, universal human security—in other words, we are not dealing with interference in our internal affairs.

First of all, I want to speak of the question of communications, which is decisive for the whole struggle for human rights in the USSR and for my public activity. The only weapon in our struggle is publicity, the open and free word. Inside our country, all channels of mass information are in the hands of the party-state apparatus. During this era of détente and a broadening struggle for human rights, ties with the West, acquisition in the West of information about violations of human rights, and the most effective, exact utilization of this information have acquired enormous importance. Authorities in the USSR undertake the most brazen measures to cut off channels of communication with the West, and it seems to me that only by actively opposing this can we anticipate successful cooperation in the struggle for human rights.

Are you aware that hundreds of people wishing to emigrate do not receive the required invitations from abroad, invitations which the authorities always arbitrarily require, in violation of the right of free choice of country of residence? Because of this, such people are not even officially included in the number of those wishing to emigrate. Many of those with relatives abroad are deprived of the opportunity to talk with them. Letters, telegrams, books, packages, and other international postal materials do not reach addresses. The authorities temporarily or permanently shut off the telephones of people who allegedly have undesirable international conversations over the telephone, thereby making it clear that the KGB listens to conversations.

Even the invitation to today's meeting was marked by such violations. Nadezhda Mandelshtam, Aleksandr Podrabinek, Anatoly Marchenko,† and I did not receive letters with invitations. Rather, I received an envelope with a mocking drawing of the extinct monster brontosaurus. The KGB evidently had in mind those they call reactionaries—perhaps you, Mr. Meany, and, of course, me. But in fact, the real brontosaurus is the repressive system which spawns such illegalities. The morning of November 27, after already having discussed the missing invitation aloud with my wife in our thoroughly KGB-bugged apartment, I finally received your invitation.

What actions do we expect from you?

· Facilitation of a broad campaign in the press and in

Congress against violations of the freedom to exchange information.

· Facilitation of the solution of this question on the level of intergovernmental negotiations.

· Measures to increase the effectiveness of radio broadcasts to the Soviet Union and the countries of Eastern Europe. In particular, it is very important that the Voice of America have its own permanent representative in the USSR, so that this station can transmit—more often, in full, and without annoying distortions—the documents it receives on human-rights violations.

· Attainment of unhindered, international television broadcasts from communications satellites.

I rely upon the AFL–CIO to continue its active support of the struggle for free choice of country of residence, because in my view this is a key problem in the larger struggle for individual freedom from the arbitrariness of the state. I remember with gratitude President Meany's decisive speeches in support of the Jackson-Vanik Amendment.

The following eminent participants in the human rights movement are now in prison or exile in the USSR: Sergei Kovalev, Semyon Gluzman, Anatoly Marchenko, Andrei Tverdokhlebov, Malva Landa, Mykola Rudenko, Oleksei Tykhy, and many others. Awaiting trial are Gamsakhurdia, Gajauskas, Ginzburg, Kostava, Marynovych, Matusevych, Orlov, Pailodze, Petkus, and Shcharansky. The priests Vins and Romanyuk, many dozens of religious believers, and Igor Ogurtsov, the leader of the All-Russia Social Christian Association for the Liberation of Peoples (VSKhSON), are in prison. Many who have tried to leave the country—participants in the so-called Leningrad airplane case, Zosimov, Fedorenko,† and dozens of others—are in detention or in psychiatric prisons, on the illegal charge of treason to their country.

It should be a matter of honor for America to achieve the release of the Ukrainian artist Pyotr Ruban, convicted for preparing a commemorative present—a wooden bookcover with a model of the Statue of Liberty—as a gift to the

American people in honor of the 200th anniversary of their independence.

Recently, the Association of American Scientists and Engineers working in the field of computer technology adopted the decision to end contacts with their colleagues in the USSR if Anatoly Shcharansky should be convicted. I expect similar steps in the case of unjustified rejection of requests by Slepak, Meiman, Goldfarb, and many others to emigrate. I consider that steps such as rejection of contacts are justified in the struggle for each individual human life and fate.

Détente is not only the attempt, through establishing contacts, trade, and technological and cultural ties, to weaken the threat of universal destruction. It is also the complex, many-sided antagonism of two systems against each other, at the basis of which lies the contradiction between totalitarianism and democracy, between violations of human rights and their observance, between the striving to close society and the striving to open it. On the outcome of this struggle depends the convergence of our societies— which is the alternative to the collapse of civilization and to general destruction.

Since the time of the Helsinki Conference, which officially proclaimed this mutual interdependence, the struggle for human rights has been constantly strengthened. America can be proud that its President proclaimed the defense of human rights as the moral basis for U.S. policy. New forms in the struggle for human rights have arisen in Czechoslovakia, Poland, and other countries in Eastern Europe. In Western countries, the ideas of this struggle increasingly penetrate public consciousness, uniting the most varied people, from conservatives to Eurocommunists. A few days ago we heard, with a feeling of profound joy, of the political amnesty in Yugoslavia, the first, to our knowledge, in the history of socialist countries. This daring and humane step is evidence of an irreversible moral victory of the ideology of human rights over the ideology of totalitarianism. Now the governments of other countries— from the USSR to Indonesia—should follow suit!

I am convinced that the AFL–CIO, with its enormous

influence upon the domestic and international policy of the U.S.A., can become one of the centers which coordinates and directs actions in defense of human rights throughout the world, and thereby in defense of our common future. Thank you for your attention.

Afterword

I intend here to deal anew, but in summary fashion, with some of the main issues already treated in many of the documents in this collection. One of them is my evaluation of the role of the human-rights movement in the USSR and Eastern Europe and my thoughts on the attitude of the West to the human-rights question. I also intend to discuss international and domestic problems, including the issue of disarmament, the East-West political and military confrontation, repressions and other human-rights violations in the USSR, and some social matters. I am obliged, however, to deal with most of these problems all too cursorily.

Opponents of the human-rights movement in the USSR and Eastern Europe often advance the following arguments:

1. These people ("those who think differently") represent no one. They are loners, alienated, disillusioned and embittered people.

2. For the bulk of the population, social welfare is the primary concern, and in that area, supposedly, the socialist countries far surpass the capitalist ones, particularly in the fields of free medical care, education, etc.

3. The central question for our times is the attainment of peace through détente and arms-control negotiations on the one hand and the advancement of the military and economic power of the socialist countries—the "bulwark of peace"—on the other. By injecting their concocted problems into this pursuit, the "dissenters" play into the hands of Cold War advocates.

4. The dissenters are not fighting for real rights for the broad mass of the people, but only for the little bunch of fellow-thinkers who have gotten into trouble. Those who stand up today to protest the violation of the rights of political prisoners in camps will be sitting in the camps themselves tomorrow, and new victims-to-be will be defending them. This struggle ends up being senseless—in the broadest meaning—since it simply perpetuates the chain of repression and protest, does real damage to social stability, provokes suffering, and creates "make-work" for the KGB.

5. The attention given dissenters by the Western press is greatly exaggerated, out of all proportion to their real significance.

What can be said of such arguments? They *may* seem persuasive, but they are based not on life's profound truths, but at best on half-truths mixed with the lies and accompanying propaganda of a totalitarian state. The arguments reflect the decades-long distortion of concepts and principles which that state has created.

Dissenters—whether dissidents, religious believers, or would-be emigrants—are often victimized by repression in a state with very little respect for justice and the rule of law and a tradition of exceptional cruelty in a camp and prison system which doubles as an important source of manpower. It is completely natural that the defense of prisoners of conscience and the attempts to help them and their families should be a basic element—though not a goal in itself—of the defense of human rights. It is certainly not the fault of the dissenters if the nature of our state leads the authorities to punish such activity as severely as the worst common crimes. Dissenters are the last to seek this victimization. (Indeed, in many cases I consider that emigration or a withdrawal from active involvement in dissent is not only justified but essential for those who, under our conditions, are certain to face the Hobson's choice of imprisonment or psychiatric confinement. In this category are many former inmates who are released only to be saddled by the authorities with illegal and inhuman probation regulations, those who are kept on a psychiatric register, and certain others.)

Of course dissenters are few; how could it be otherwise in a state where everyone is either a hired hand of the government or a functionary, and all live in total dependence on the state? Dissenters cannot be called generals without armies, for they are neither generals nor officers of any army at all. They represent only themselves, their own free thinking and their own consciences. But in a totalitarian monolithic setting that is already a great deal. Theirs is a qualitative leap, liberating the consciousness of millions of people, of those who come home from work every day to twist the dials of their transistor radios. Their activity is of interest to the whole world after decades of living next to the totalitarian colossus.

The West has finally begun to pay attention to dissent. If millions of loyal citizens fell silent victims to organized famine and furious repression in the '30s and '40s—and the West as a whole (governments, the mass media, and most of the intelligentsia) said nothing—then in the '60s and '70s silence became an impossibility. That has been one result of the heroic struggle for public notice of a few hundred dissenters out of a population of hundreds of millions. We are convinced that knowledge of the real situation in the USSR and Eastern Europe—as in the rest of the world—is a practical necessity for the West, first of all. The defense of victims of repression, of civil and political rights, is an essential foundation of the pursuit of international stability and confidence. Although this concept is receiving wider and wider recognition, further efforts are still needed to have it completely realized in practice. Many public figures in the West have already understood this truth, but still, and especially among policymakers, there persists a short-sighted pragmatism—a frivolous hope of obtaining instantaneous solutions for the most complex problems of peace and justice and, on occasion, banal political intriguing to exploit burning human-rights problems on which mankind's fate depends.

As to the charge that dissenters and their human-rights campaign impede détente and progress toward peace, the main theme of my public activity since its very start has been the unquestioned priority that problems of peace and disarmament have in our age of nuclear weapons. It is wrong to accept the contention of the Soviet press and of some shortsighted Westerners that the pursuit of peace and the human-rights movement are mutually contradictory. I will not go into the "glowing" passages of the Soviet press on this theme, as they contain no serious attempt at reasoning.

Not long ago, we in the Soviet Union heard radio broadcasts of the comments of several American and European papers on the results of Secretary Vance's visit to Moscow in April 1978. A majority of the commentators agreed that a year before, President Carter's firm human-rights policy had been the main reason for the breakdown of the SALT talks with Foreign Minister Gromyko and that the progress achieved (the scale of which was unknown, but the comments cited the optimistic tone of official statements) was somehow the result of a "softening" or "erosion" of Carter's position. To me such analyses exemplify the myopic pragmatism and superficiality to which I refer. They stand logic on its head and stab the human-rights campaign in the back.

As I said in the April 4, 1977, interview with Swedish radio, the complications which showed up in the SALT negotiations last year are profound issues which could not be sidestepped. They are linked to fundamental flaws in the Vladivostok agreement, to traditional peculiarities of Soviet politics, and to certain technical issues—but not in any way to the problems of human rights.

Then and now I perceive the 1977 negotiations as in no sense a failure of American policy; they clearly demonstrated the dynamic and constructive character of the U.S. position, contributed to a degree in delivering the West from certain dangerous illusions, and created the basis for further talks and major decisions. It seems obvious to me that a firm policy on human rights could not and cannot "spoil" anything. On the contrary, it shows that the West will not succumb to blackmail, feelings of weakness and uncertainty, that it will resolutely defend the principles which hold such fundamental significance for our common future. Weakness or excessive "flexibility" on human-rights matters immediately undermines Western positions all along the détente "front."

Disarmament negotiations have their own substantive significance. The fact that they are underway diminishes to some extent the likelihood that a major war will break out. They cannot, however, eliminate the reasons for polit-ico-military opposition. When they bring about some limi-tation on military outlays, that is important, but unfortu-nately such limitation appears to be a reality mainly in the West. Until now no agreed restraints, as far as I know, have been able to compel the Soviet military-industrial complex to renounce even one projected weapons system or cut back the numerical strength of its army, air force, tanks, artillery, and strategic missiles. I am speaking here of real reductions, not so-called ceilings on forces. In these circumstances the West must complement arms negotia-tions by a concern for strengthening its armaments. The situation is especially dangerous in Europe, where the im-balance of forces is promoting a subtle economic and po-litical dependence on the USSR.

The confrontational aspects of Soviet policy that are most alarming are the efforts to gain military superiority in many parts of the world, the drive to expand spheres of influence, especially in strategic locales, and the support for the most dangerous international forces. The systematic buildup of armed strength—tanks, multiple-warhead mis-siles, the world's strongest submarine fleet—is being syn-chronized with a noisy, demagogic campaign against the neutron bomb. (The neutron bomb is, more precisely, an enhanced-radiation weapon. It is no more humane than any other weapon, but it is primarily defensive. It has only localized effect and is meant for use against tanks and columns of armored transport in thickly populated regions, especially in Europe, where unthinking people and their leaders have been led by prejudices and incitement to allow NATO tank strength to lag repeatedly behind that of the USSR and its allies.)

No matter how important arms-control discussions are, they can produce decisive results only when they are joined to the resolution of broader and more complicated problems of military-political and ideological confrontation, including questions of human rights. The freedom to exchange information at home and across international borders, the freedom to move at home and to travel or emigrate abroad, all rank as prerequisites of international trust, basic to the process of diminishing hostility. As long as a country has no civil liberty, no freedom of information, and no independent press, then there exists no effective body of public opinion to control the conduct of the government and its functionaries. Such a situation is not just a misfortune for citizens unprotected against tyranny and lawlessness; it is a menace to international security.

Having no arguments to use in dealing with questions of civil rights and political liberty, Soviet and pro-Soviet propagandists usually try to divert the discussion to the issue of welfare and so-called social rights. But, in fact, the situation in these areas is no better. It is only harder to comprehend this truth from a distance than it is in the case of such clear violations as those of the rights of foreign journalists. It is even difficult for those who live in the country to judge the truth, because statistical data are not published and anything which might produce a "bad" impression is censored. In *My Country and the World,* I tried —without pretending to offer a really profound analysis—to give a picture of the way our social system looks from the inside. Very little has changed in recent years. The average monthly salary has increased somewhat (according to official figures, up to 150 rubles—even higher if social security and benefit payments are counted in), but this rise has been eaten up by the accompanying sharp growth of hidden inflation. (One form of the hidden inflation is the acute deterioration of the quality of consumer goods kept on sale at their old prices, even while better-quality wares remain available in the special stores reserved for the bosses. Of course, the prices of some items have gone way up; coffee, for example, has risen by four and a half times.)

There is something interesting for Western readers in the supposedly free system of medical care: both those who stay home when ill and those who are hospitalized have to obtain their medicine themselves. I will not even speak of the mass of unofficial expenses an ordinary patient must meet. Other alarming aspects of our existence have not only persisted but grown more pronounced: pervasive drunkenness, general petty corruption, the decline in respect—especially among young people—for intellectual careers in teaching and medicine, the rise in crime, discord among nationalities, the cruel and often unjust judicial system, the bureaucratic apparatus, the fragmentation of society into castes. Not long ago the Helsinki Watch Group published documents on the situation of pensioners and invalids, based on a careful study of an enormous number of laws, regulations, and other documents. I strongly recommend their findings to the reader. In my view the West needs to have a detailed understanding of our population's real social situation in order to dispel the myths of Soviet propaganda and clear up the reality. Without such knowledge, moreover, it would be difficult to comprehend anything about our life, about the internal and foreign policy of the USSR, about the prospects for socialism in other countries, and about similar issues.

A number of important events in the campaign for human rights have marked 1977 and 1978. The ideas of that struggle have continued to grow and spread, and the struggle itself has taken on new forms. Among other international occurrences the Belgrade Meeting gave human-rights questions a central place. An unquestionable spirit of tactical and philosophical kinship animated the growth of the human-rights movement in Czechoslovakia (the splendid Charter '77), in Poland (the Workers' Defense Committee and others), and in the USSR (the Helsinki Watch Groups). Even though all this occurred without any organizational ties or contacts, it is now possible to speak of a united movement in the Soviet Union and Eastern Europe. The Eurocommunists of Spain, Italy, and France have assumed a new position on human rights. In the United States, President Carter used his Inaugural Address to proclaim that the defense of human rights the world over would be the moral foundation of American policy. Amnesty International was awarded the 1977 Nobel Peace Prize. And the political amnesties in Yugoslavia, Indonesia, and Chile represented even more tangible expressions of the victory of human-rights thinking.

Nonetheless, political repression, ethnic and religious persecution, and other human-rights violations have simultaneously continued and even intensified in a number of countries. (Here I am referring to certain recent occurrences which are not covered by material in this collection. In it I write only about what goes on in the Soviet Union, not what I know of from the radio or from newspapers.) There can be no forgetting the suffering and deaths of many, the massive violation of human rights in various nations—Cambodia, Vietnam, Uganda, Brazil, several other African and Central and South American countries, Iran; the list is a long one.

Levko Lukyanenko, a member of the Helsinki Watch Group who has already served a fifteen-year term of political imprisonment, has been arrested in the Ukraine. In Armenia two Helsinki Watch Group members—Robert Nazarian and Shagen Arutunian—have been arrested, the latter on the false felony charge of resisting arrest. In Georgia two members — Valentina Pailodze and Viktor Rtskhiladze —have been jailed, as has Avtandil Imnadze. Helsinki Watch Group member Pyotr Vins,† the son of the imprisoned Baptist religious leader Georgy Vins,† has himself been sentenced to a year of incarceration on a trumped-up charge of parasitism, "refusal to engage in socially productive labor." Grigory Goldshtein,† a scientist and inventor, has been sentenced to the same term on the same charge, but in fact because of his participation in the Georgian Helsinki Watch Group and his desire to emigrate to Israel. The same accusation—widely used as a reprisal against anyone of whom the authorities disapprove—has been used to convict Ivan Vagner, a worker with thirty-two years of labor to his credit who had sought to emigrate to West Germany. Mykola Matusevych† and Myroslav Marynovych,† both Ukrainian Helsinki Watchers, have each been sentenced in Kiev to seven years in prison camps and five years of internal exile. In Lithuania, Balys Gajauskas† has been given a hideously cruel sentence of ten years' imprisonment and five years' exile for participating in the fund to aid political prisoners, despite his having already served over twenty-five years (1949–76) in the Stalin-era and post-Stalin camps. Six members of the Seventh-Day Adventist congregation have been arrested in Tashkent, the latest victims in the long-running official persecution of this sect for its independent religious stance. Among those jailed is the sect's eighty-three-year-old spiritual leader, Vladimir Shelkov, who has already undergone twenty-three years of imprisonment. Right after the Belgrade Meeting ended, we learned of the Supreme Soviet's Presidium decrees citing groundless charges to revoke the citizenship of Major General Pyotr Grigorenko,† one of the finest leaders in the human-rights movement and an honored wartime commander and World War II invalid, and of the world-renowned cellist Mstislav Rostropovich and his wife, Galina Vishnevskaya. For his public statements, Grigorenko, who was a member of both the Moscow and Ukrainian Helsinki Watch Groups, had already been stripped of his military rank and condemned to spend more than four years in insane asylums.

As it has for many years, the persecution of Baptists, Pentecostals, and members of other independent religious communities continues, as do the oppression of and discrimination against Crimean Tatars seeking only the right to live in the Crimea, and a variety of national, religious, and other repression. Hundreds of political prisoners—to whose number these past months have been added Ukrainian Helsinki Watchers Mykola Rudenko† and Oleksei Tykhy† for seven- and ten-year camp terms, respectively, as well as five years of exile—continue their path of struggle and suffering in the camps, prisons, and psychiatric hospitals, subjected daily to cold and hunger, to backbreaking labor, to restrictions on their rights to meet and correspond with their families, and to other arbitrary treatment.

The freedom to choose the country where one lives is another right which continues to be severely limited, even though such restrictions amount to direct violations of the Human Rights Covenants and the Helsinki Accord. These violations damage international confidence and mutual understanding, as well as victimizing Jews, Germans, Ukrainians, Russians, Lithuanians, Armenians, and people of other nationalities.

I have named the Helsinki Watch Group members arrested and convicted in recent months, but Yuri Orlov,† Aleksandr Ginzburg,† Zviad Gamsakhurdia,† and Merab Kostava† have been held without trial for more than a year, and Viktoras Petkus† was arrested over nine months ago. Among the thirty-five nations of the Helsinki Accord guaranteeing respect for human rights, the rulers of those states where rights are systematically violated have employed special tactics to repress those men and women who linked their names and civic action to Helsinki. The immediate goal of those tactics is to stem the flow of information, but that goal is unattainable. The repression, accordingly, can be called a bureaucratic reflex. In the USSR the mechanistic soullessness of political persecution makes it especially cruel and unjust, particularly when little-known people or second-time political offenders are its objects.

At present, however, the KGB "brains trust" seems to me to be pursuing an even wider aim. By arresting Helsinki Watch Group members and sentencing some of them with a cruelty no one could fail to notice, the Soviet authorities were issuing a defiant challenge to the Western Helsinki signatories and Belgrade Meeting participants. They were confronting them with the painful dilemma of either defending the Helsinki principles with uncompromising demands for the liberation of all those arrested—thereby risking heightened tension with the East—or capitulating, backing off from the challenge and thus weakening their positions not only in human-rights matters, not only at Belgrade, but in all aspects of détente.

As an added benefit—even if the ploy were a partial failure—the authorities could count on these "fresh" repressions to draw attention away from the other, massive and permanent human-rights violations in the USSR. What must never be overlooked is the fact that the entire tactic is a bluff. After all, it is the Soviets who have the most at stake in the aspects of Helsinki not connected to human rights, and the West which has the primary interest in the free flow of information and people as well as other civil and political liberties. Although I and other dissidents have repeatedly expressed these ideas in a whole series of documents, it seems fitting to voice them once again here.

The closing of the Belgrade Meeting brought one episode of the Helsinki drama to an end. This is not the place for a detailed evaluation of its effect on the socialist and Western countries and of the Meeting's overall significance. The flabby stance taken by a number of major European states on the human-rights issue at Belgrade and the lack of any direct mention of the problem in the concluding document was certainly disappointing. Nevertheless, I view the session as an enormously important event with far-reaching consequences. For the first time, specific human-rights violations were discussed at such a representative international level, and the discussion drew the attention of the press, public figures, and world opinion. Despite some slip-ups and compromises, the West in general made it very plain that observance of human rights is a matter of fundamental significance and will remain a central issue. The permanence of human-rights concerns was a key feature of the decision of the delegates to meet again in Madrid in 1980.

In this new phase, on the eve of the next series of trials of Helsinki Watch Group members, I now again call on society, Western political leaders, and those involved in cultural, scientific, trade, and technological contacts with the USSR and Eastern Europe to follow closely the reports on human-rights violations there and do all in their power to prevent and correct them. It is essential to employ all possible leverage—discreet and public diplomacy, the press, demonstrations and other means that strike at prestige, boycotts, cancellations of cooperative activities in one field or another, legislative limitations on trade and contacts similar to the Jackson-Vanik Amendment, prisoner exchanges—to save the individual victims of tyranny and lawlessness and entire categories of people suffering injustice and discrimination, to reverse the practice of arbitrary rule.

I must again emphasize the importance of defending all the arrested members of the Helsinki Watch Groups. Under the circumstances, their defense is the touchstone of Western resoluteness and perseverance as well as a test of the good faith and reasonableness of the Soviet side. This is a major international affair. In all the campaigns of support it is terribly important not to divide the arrested and convicted into separate categories—the important ones for whom it is easy to generate backing and publicity and the secondary figures whom the authorities count on dealing with in silence as they wish. I appeal for the creation of a unified international committee to defend all Helsinki Watch Group members, to bring together the forces of several groups already at work.

In connection with prisoner exchanges, I wholeheartedly supported the exchange of Luis Corvalan and Vladimir Bukovsky.† It was a wise and compassionate act which granted freedom to two men. I hope for further exchanges to save those who are gravely ill, women, and political prisoners subjected to especially severe injustice. I consider the exchanges as humanitarian actions standing apart from either political or strictly juridical considerations. Unfortunately, it is true that in the West there is a different opinion, a legalistic one, which opposes exchanges. There are supporters of this stance even in such impartial and humanitarian organizations as Amnesty International. All of them fail, I think, to appreciate just how difficult it is to tear a man from imprisonment in a totalitarian state and what a great good fortune it is to succeed in doing so. Since exchanges of prisoners are not commercial deals, there is no need to worry about making them precisely balanced. For that reason, it comes as bitter news to me to hear that official State Department representatives consider Anatoly Shcharansky's† innocence of espionage charges a possible obstacle to arranging an exchange for him.

To my mind, the main significance of this collection is in its documentary character, the full and accurate presentation of original materials accompanied by the compiler's comprehensive commentary. Such a publication is especially important for us, given the conditions in our country which deny us much of the access enjoyed in nontotalitarian states to communications and published material.

Most of the documents included in this collection are ones I transmitted to the West with the aim of having them printed in the press there and with the hope that they would be carried on foreign radio broadcasts. Those programs represent almost the only source of information for people in our country on the problems which our official information media pass over in silence. Unfortunately, I— like many of my friends, for whom, like me, publicity is the only means of civic action—experience enduring hardships and disappointments in the collaboration with Western media so vital to us. Too often our announcements disappear without a trace, sometimes even when they deal with the most tragic cases; sometimes they are published in incorrect or seriously distorted versions. Then Western radio broadcasts, relaying these mistakes, end up by misinforming millions of people: the names of the persecuted are dropped, the most important details are overlooked. Sometimes pure negligence is to blame. Our fight for public attention takes place in the most difficult of circumstances and involves heavy sacrifices. It is intolerable to have frivolous causes spoil even a part of the fruits of our struggle. I have written and spoken about this problem repeatedly, particularly since my own public activity was so greatly impeded when the authorities cut off my international telephone conversations in 1974.

This collection, of course, cannot have the immediacy of radio or newsprint. Today the majority of the documents have a somewhat retrospective character. Nevertheless, because of its completeness and accuracy, the collection seems to me useful and necessary.

I am writing as the world recoils from the monstrous, cold-blooded murder of Aldo Moro, one of Italy's best men. The West has much to worry about; life is difficult, tragic, in no sense unclouded even there. I know that, and I feel it today more acutely than ever. But I know something else as well: most of the problems and tragedies which occur in the West, like those in totalitarian countries, affect all of mankind. Events like the murder of Moro shock and shake those of us who are denied democratic freedoms no less than those whose democracy is under explosive assault from the Red Brigades and other terrorists. In truth we are all united by a common goal; in that is our faith and our hope.

MOSCOW,
May 11, 1978

Biographical Appendix

Below, in alphabetical order, appear brief supplementary sketches of some of the individuals whom Sakharov sought to publicize and defend, and details about their cases.

Paruir Airikian, an Armenian nationalist, was first arrested in 1969 at the age of twenty and sentenced to four years in a camp for organizing an illegal group to study Armenian history, culture, and language. In 1973 he returned to Erevan but was arrested a year later and sentenced to two years in labor camp for violating the rules of administrative surveillance. While serving that sentence he was tried once again on a new charge of anti-Soviet propaganda in the autumn of 1974 and sentenced to seven years in a strict-regime camp and three years in exile. In court he announced that he had been a member of the National United Party of Armenia since 1967 and continued to support its goals and program since it advocated self-determination for Armenia in accordance with the Soviet Constitution.

Ivan Vasilevich Biblenko, like Nikolai Nikolaevich Deinega and Yaroslav Ivanovich Shkraba (q.v.), was a member of the Evangelical Christian-Baptist Church. The three of them have died in controversial circumstances in unrelated incidents. Baptist dissenters believe that they and many of their fellow believers were murdered by the authorities.

Unlike the official Baptist Church, their sect refuses to register its congregations with state authorities, and its members are often imprisoned for this illegal conduct.

Biblenko was forty-seven years old when, on September 13, 1975, he left his family in the city of Krivoi Rog to attend a harvest festival celebration in Dnepropetrovsk. A religious activist who had served one term of imprisonment for infringing anti-proselytization laws, Biblenko—the police told his relatives after the latter began to search for him on September 16—had been under surveillance when he left for the harvest ceremony. Until his wife and mother were notified on September 26 that Biblenko had died in the Mechnikov Hospital in Dnepropetrovsk, police and traffic officials denied to the women having any knowledge of his whereabouts and claimed that no traffic accidents had occurred on the road between the two cities on either September 13 or 14. The hospital certificate, however, showed that Biblenko had been admitted September 17, having suffered a fractured skull "in a traffic-related accident" on September 13. Although the cause of death was given as pneumonia and hemorrhaging of the brain, twenty-nine members of the Krivoi Rog unofficial Baptist community signed a statement alleging: "People deliberately beat Biblenko to the point where it was certain that he would not live. Then they took him to the hospital on the verge of death, and his relatives were not permitted to see him alive so that he could not tell them what had happened to him nor expose the evil-doing."

Konstantin Bogatyrev, a translator of German poetry, was fifty-one when he was attacked and badly beaten on the landing outside his apartment in Moscow on April 26, 1976. He died of his injuries in a Moscow hospital on June 18, and his assailant has not yet been found. Although no evidence suggests that officials sanctioned the fatal attack, it is known that Bogatyrev had been given a "strong warning" by the Moscow section of the Union of Writers in May 1968 for signing petitions defending Aleksandr Ginzburg and Yuri Galanskov, who were tried that year. He also wrote the Secretariat of the Moscow branch of his union in February 1974 to protest its expulsion of the satirist Vladimir Voinovich.

Igor Brusnikin, who lived in the village of Sayan in the Dzhezkazganskaya oblast, was arrested on May 27, 1975, two days after a street fight—common in the region—between Kazakh and Russian youths. His death a month after his arrest was the result of injuries suffered during interrogation, according to his mother. A photograph of the corpse shows Brusnikin's hands covered with stab wounds, and, according to his mother, similar wounds covered the rest of his body as well. The mother, Galina Petrovna Brusnikina, asserts on the basis of his cellmates' (Polienko and Chevard) testimony that Brusnikin had to be carried back to his cell after each interrogation.

Vladimir Bukovsky was first confined to a psychiatric hospital for his political views in 1963. He was forcibly recommitted in late 1965 for helping to organize what was to be the first post-Stalin public protest by Moscow dissenters, the Pushkin Square demonstration of December 5, 1965, to demand that any trial of the writers Andrei Sinyavsky and Yuli Daniel be open to all. Released from the insane asylum after a few months, he was seized at another protest demonstration on January 22, 1967, and sentenced to three years in the camps. After his release he spent approximately a year compiling the first extensive documentation on the use of Soviet psychiatry against political and other nonconformists, sent it to the West in March 1971, and was sentenced—ten months later—to a term of two years in prison, five in camp, and five in exile. Under the steady pressure of Western public indignation, Soviet authorities finally consented in December 1976 to exchange Bukovsky for imprisoned Chilean Communist Party leader Luis Corvalan. The swap took place in Zurich, Switzerland, where Bukovsky was flown in handcuffs, directly from Vladimir Prison. The exchange was hailed as a Soviet admission that the USSR *does* hold political prisoners—not just common criminals—and by Sakharov (see the Afterword) as a first step toward liberating Bukovsky's many fellow prisoners of conscience. In February 1977, Bukovsky became the first Soviet dissident to be received by a President at the White House.

Vyacheslav Chornovil, Ukrainian journalist, born January 1, 1938, was arrested in 1967 for having smuggled out to the West and published the *Chornovil Papers* (McGraw-Hill, New York, 1968), an early collection of *samizdat* protests against Soviet suppression of Ukrainian culture. He was sentenced again in 1972 for "anti-Soviet propaganda" to five years' strict regime, three years' internal exile.

Nikolai Nikolaevich Deinega, a Baptist villager in the Ukrainian province of Chernigov, was murdered at a bus stop on September 9, 1976, at the age of 57. He had been subjected to persecution by local authorities since he and his wife and children had formally sought to emigrate from the USSR.

Vasily Fedorenko, a plumber, born March 30, 1928, in the Chernigov oblast, had served two previous prison-camp terms before he was caught fleeing to the West in September 1974, after having been refused permission to emigrate to West Germany to join his sister. He was sentenced in March 1975 to five years of prison and ten years of special-regimen camp on treason charges of "betrayal of the motherland" and for "anti-Soviet agitation and propaganda." According to the Uzhgorod City Court's verdict, Fedorenko ". . . after his release [he had last left camp in the autumn of 1972] . . . continued to spread anti-Soviet fabrications among his co-workers. . . . he approved of actions by Solzhenitsyn and Sakharov which were harmful for the Soviet Union, furthermore, he stated that the Soviet authorities were unjustly repressing them. . . . the slander was directed first of all against the Communist Party of the Soviet Union, against the Soviet government, against the working class, and against the friendship of the peoples of the Soviet Union. . . . he escaped across the border . . . with the intention of asking asylum in a capitalist country and to conduct on its territory activity hostile to the socialist countries with the purpose of liquidating Soviet rule on the territory of the Soviet Union." Fedorenko conducted a hunger strike as soon as he was delivered to Vladimir Prison in April 1975, and was still being force-fed there in December 1976.

Yuri Fyodorov, one of the defendants in the Leningrad hijacking trial of December 1970, was sentenced to fifteen years of special-regimen camp, although he said at the trial that all the accused had "one single aim—to leave the USSR." He had served a previous term for "anti-Soviet agitation and propaganda."

Balys Gajauskas, a Lithuanian, had served half of his fifty years in prison and forced-labor camp for his advocacy of Lithuanian nationalism when he was released in 1976. He engaged in editorial work for the underground *Chronicle of the Lithuanian Church* and administered monies from the "Russian Social Fund" founded by Solzhenitsyn to aid political prisoners, until he was arrested in April 1977 for "anti-Soviet propaganda." He was convicted in April 1978, and sentenced to ten years in a labor camp and five years of internal exile.

Zviad Gamsakhurdia, a Georgian, born in 1939, was a writer and lecturer on English literature at Tbilisi University, a member of Amnesty International, a founder of the Georgian Helsinki Watch Group, and editor of two *samizdat* journals. He was arrested on April 7, 1977, and sent in the fall of 1977 to Moscow's Serbsky Institute for "psychiatric" examination. He was tried in May 1978 and sentenced to three years in a labor camp and two years of internal exile—a lighter sentence than that given Helsinki Watchers elsewhere in the USSR, and one he is thought to have earned by recanting at least some of his views in court and on Soviet television.

Aleksandr Ginzburg, born November 21, 1936, member of the Moscow Helsinki Watch Group and administrator of Solzhenitsyn's prisoners aid fund, was arrested in February 1977 and sentenced in July 1978 to eight years in a special-regimen labor camp on charges of anti-Soviet propaganda. Ginzburg had edited the *samizdat* literary journal *Syntax* while still a student at Moscow University, and compiled a detailed record of the 1966 trial of Andrei Sinyavsky and Yuli Daniel. Having served one prison camp term (1960–62), Ginzburg was arrested in 1967 on charges of anti-Soviet propaganda and served a five-year sentence in the labor camps.

Semyon Gluzman, born in 1946, was sentenced by the Kiev Oblast Court in December 1972 to seven years in a strict-regimen camp and three years in exile, after a number of witnesses testified that Gluzman had either shown or mentioned anti-Soviet literature to them. Many believe that the young psychiatrist was actually tried and convicted because he wrote an article refuting the finding of insanity on the basis of which General Grigorenko (q.v.) was forcibly hospitalized. In the spring of 1976, Dr. Gluzman, still in the Perm political prison camps, was threatened with a second Article 70 trial in connection with the publication in the West of *A Dissident's Guide to Psychiatry,* which Gluzman wrote in camp with Vladimir Bukovsky.

Grigory Goldshtein, a forty-seven-year-old physicist and founding member of the Georgian Helsinki Watch Group, was sentenced in

March 1978 to one year in labor camp for "parasitism." He and his brother, Isai, have long and unsuccessfully sought permission to emigrate to Israel.

Major General Pyotr Grigorevich Grigorenko, born in 1907, one of the most active and best-known Soviet human-rights activists, was held in a special psychiatric hospital from 1969 to 1975, diagnosed as suffering from "paranoid development of the personality with the presence of reformist ideas." A founder of both the Moscow and Ukrainian Helsinki Watch groups, he was stripped of Soviet citizenship while on a visit to the U.S. in 1978.

Viktor Khaustov, a worker in the Moscow electric vacuum plant, was first arrested during a demonstration in Pushkin Square in Moscow on January 22, 1967. The demonstrators were protesting the arrests of Yuri Galanskov, Alexei Dobrovolsky, Vera Lashkova, and Pavel Padzievsky. (Within a year Galanskov, Dobrovolsky, and Lashkova went on trial with Aleksandr Ginzburg on charges of "anti-Soviet agitation and propaganda"—this was the well-known "Trial of the Four.")

Another cause espoused by the demonstrators was voiced in the slogan: "We demand a review of the anticonstitutional decree and Article 70!"

Article 70 of the Criminal Code of the Russian Federation (similar or identical articles are contained in the codes of all the other republics) relates to "anti-Soviet agitation and propaganda." It penalizes such acts as the "manufacture" and "dissemination" "with the intent of undermining or weakening Soviet power" of "slanderous fabrications discrediting the Soviet social and state system, or any similar dissemination or manufacture or possession of literature of similar content with such intents."

The decree referred to in the slogan is the Decree of the Presidium of the Supreme Soviet of the R.S.F.S.R. of September 16, 1966, which introduced Articles 190.1 and 190.3 into the Criminal Code. Article 190.1 differs from Article 70 chiefly in eliminating the consideration of anti-Soviet intent in judging the actions of the accused —that is, whether it was his intention to weaken or undermine Soviet power. However, when bringing charges under either of these two articles, the authorities as a rule follow no juridical consideration. It is well known that, in the majority of political trials carried out under Article 70, the prosecution doesn't prove, or even seriously attempt to prove, the anti-Soviet intent of the accused. The sole fact of dissemination or manufacture of objectionable materials (often information concerning the violation of human rights in the U.S.S.R.) serves as sufficient proof of intent.

The constitutional freedom to assemble, march, and demonstrate was violated, in the opinion of the demonstrators, by Article 190.3: "An organization, or any similarly active participation in group ac-

tions, roughly violating the social order or attended by obvious de-
liberate disobedience of a lawfully invested representative of authority, or which interferes with the functioning of transportation,
of state or public-service institutions or of business. . . ." In accordance with this article, and for participation in this demonstration,
Viktor Khaustov was sentenced to his first prison-camp term of three
years.

Khaustov received his second term of imprisonment—four years
in a strict-regimen camp and two years of internal exile—at the hands
of the Orel City Court in March 1974. He was convicted in this case
of having given *The Chronicle of Current Events* information concerning the founding in Orel of a group which intended, so far as can
be determined, to issue a typewritten newspaper, *The Russian Pa-
triotic Front* (the three founders of this group were arrested at the
end of 1972 and sentenced to five- and four-year prison terms for
"anti-Soviet agitation and propaganda"); of having participated in a
collective appeal in defense of Bukovsky and Yakir; and of having
reproduced and sent to the West the *Prison Diaries* of the Leningrad
"hijacker" Edward Kuznetsov (q.v.). Khaustov is presently in exile in
the Tomsk region.

Mati Kiirend, a thirty-nine-year-old Estonian engineer, was active in the Estonian Democratic Movement. He was sentenced in
1975 for "anti-Soviet agitation" to five years in a strict-regimen camp.

Merab Kostava, a Georgian musicologist, born in 1939, was a
member of the Georgian Helsinki Watch Group and a founder of the
samizdat journal *The Georgian Herald*. He was arrested with Gamsakhurdia on April 7, 1977, and also sent to Serbsky Institute for
"psychiatric" examination. He was convicted in Tbilisi in May 1978
and sentenced to three years in a labor camp and two years' internal
exile.

Edward Kuznetsov was born in 1939 of a Jewish father and non-
Jewish mother. In 1961, while studying philosophy at Moscow University, he was arrested, tried, and convicted for "anti-Soviet propaganda" and spent the next seven years in labor camps and Vladimir
Prison. One of the leaders in a plan to fly a small Soviet plane to
Sweden, he was sentenced to death in December 1970 for treason (a
sentence later commuted to fifteen years' imprisonment). The Leningrad hijacking trial became a key symbol for the Soviet emigration
movement. Kuznetsov managed to smuggle out of confinement his
Prison Diaries (Stein and Day, New York, 1975). Silva Zalmanson,
Kuznetsov's wife and codefendant, was sentenced to eight years in a
labor camp, but she was released in 1974 and now lives in Israel.

Malva Landa, a fifty-seven-year-old geologist-engineer, was the
first member of the Helsinki Watch Group to go on trial, on May 16,
1977. Her room had caught fire on December 18, 1976, the day the
authorities released Vladimir Bukovsky. Landa herself suffered serious

burns. She was found guilty of criminal negligence and sentenced to two years of Siberian exile; she was amnestied in March 1978 and permitted to return to European Russia, but not to Moscow.

Stase Lukshaite, fifty-nine, a former nun, holder of a postgraduate degree in technical sciences, was a Lithuanian Catholic activist who died in late 1975. Lukshaite, who continued to teach children their catechism despite strong official pressure against the religious education of youth, was found at a crossing over the Neman River in Kaunas on the morning of October 30 in critical condition from numerous bodily injuries. Regaining consciousness in the hospital just before she died on November 5, she said that she forgave her murderer. At the inquest, her sister was told, according to issue No. 23 of *The Chronicle of the Lithuanian Catholic Church,* that "somehow a terrible thing happened. Walking up the stairs, Lukshaite slipped and hurt herself."

Kronid Lyubarsky, an astrophysicist and former scientific secretary of the Moscow Division of the All-Union Society of Astronomy and Geodesy, was arrested in January 1972 and sentenced in October, in Moscow, to five years in a strict-regimen camp for distributing *samizdat* materials, including *The Chronicle of Current Events.* He was transferred in October 1974 to Vladimir Prison until his release in January 1977. Although Lyubarsky remained under police supervision in the town of Tarusa, near Moscow, after his release, he acted as one of the administrators of the "Russian Social Fund," set up by Aleksandr Solzhenitsyn to assist political prisoners and their families, until threats of new arrest forced him to emigrate in late 1977. He now lives with his wife in Munich.

Mikhail Makarenko fled from anti-Semitism in his native Romania in 1939 (at the age of eight), lied about his age in order to fight in the Red Army at the end of the war, and was arrested ten times and forcibly committed to psychiatric care four times between 1948 and July 1969, when he was imprisoned again for his energetic role in organizing exhibitions of nonconformist artists, including an attempt to show the works of Marc Chagall. In September 1970 a Moscow City Court sentenced him to eight years in a strict-regimen camp on charges of "anti-Soviet agitation and propaganda" and of various criminal acts, among them "foreign currency violations" and "working at a forbidden trade." From September 1974 until his release in July 1977, he was confined in Vladimir Prison.

Anatoly Marchenko, since his first political conviction (treason, for an attempt to flee to Iran) in March 1961 at the age of twenty-three, has spent twice as much time in prison, prison camp, and Siberian exile as at liberty. A self-educated laborer, this Siberian-born railroad worker's son is best known in the West as the author of *My Testimony* (Dutton, New York, 1969), the first account (and still among the most powerful) of conditions in the post-Stalin prison system. This book and Marchenko's other writings—including a prescient warning in July 1968 to Czechoslovak newspapers of the imminence of Soviet intervention—brought him a new term in labor camps of three years in addition to his first six. Released in 1971, Marchenko moved back to Tarusa, near Moscow, in 1972, where KGB officials resumed efforts to persuade him to apply for emigration to Israel—a common tactic for sending dissenters (even non-Jewish ones) into permanent exile. Marchenko refused the gambit, but the strict "surveillance" (a form of probation) imposed on him in 1974 drove him to renounce Soviet citizenship and apply for emigration to the United States. Arrested in February 1975 for alleged violation of his probation—the terms of which required him, among other things, not to leave his house after 8:00 p.m., even to take his young son for a walk before bed—he was sentenced to four more years of Siberian exile in the town of Chuna. However, although now approaching the end of his term of exile, Marchenko possibly will not be freed. According to the latest information, the local authorities are trying to fabricate charges of gold speculation against him.

Myroslav Marynovych, a twenty-nine-year-old engineer and editor of technical publications, was a member of the Helsinki Watch Group of the Ukraine. He was arrested on April 23, 1977. Convicted in March 1978, he was sentenced to seven years in a labor camp and five years' internal exile on charges of anti-Soviet propaganda.

Mykola Matusevych, a thirty-two-year-old worker (expelled from university history studies), was a member of the Ukrainian Helsinki Watch Group. He was arrested on April 23, 1977, with Marynovych, convicted along with him in March 1978, and sentenced to the same term of seven years in a labor camp and five years' internal exile.

Valentin Moroz, a Ukrainian historian, served four years (1965–69) of a five-year term for anti-Soviet agitation and propaganda but was arrested again in June 1970 as the author of several literary works, including the widely read *Report from the Beria Preserve* (Chicago: Cataract Press, 1974). Moroz was sentenced to five years in prison, three years in a special-regimen camp, and five years' exile, but in 1974—after a Vladimir Prison cellmate wounded him with a knife—he was put in a solitary cell, where he conducted a 145-day hunger strike. During the summer of 1976, Moroz underwent psychiatric examination at the Serbsky Institute, and after a loud public outcry in the West was declared sane and sent to a Mordovian special-regimen camp.

Igor Vyacheslavovich Ogurtsov, an orientalist born in 1937, was arrested in February 1967 in Leningrad and sentenced that November as the leader of the All-Russian Christian Social Union for the Liberation of the People (VSKhSON) to fifteen years of imprisonment and five years of exile. (On VSKhSON, see John Dunlop, *The New Russian Revolutionaries,* Belmont, Mass.: Nordland, 1976.) In all, some sixty people were arrested in connection with VSKhSON;

twenty-one were convicted in two trials. Ogurtsov and the three tried with him were found to be the organizers and leaders of the union and convicted of treason for planning an armed uprising, although the union's arsenal apparently consisted of only one rusted gun and a number of books, especially the works of the philosopher Berdyayev. Ogurtsov spent the first seven years of his term in the Vladimir Prison. He was sent in March 1974 to Perm strict-regimen Camp 35 but was soon transferred to the hospital zone of the Mordovian political prison camps with the diagnosis of "rheumatism of the brain," as reported in Perm Camp 36.

Yuri Orlov, born in 1924, a distinguished high-energy physicist, corresponding member of the Armenian Academy of Sciences and founder and chairman of the Moscow Helsinki Watch Group, was arrested in February 1977 and tried in May 1978 on charges of anti-Soviet propaganda. He was convicted and sentenced to seven years in a labor camp and five years of internal exile, despite strong support from Western physicists and human-rights organizations.

Vladimir Osipov, a forty-year-old Russian, was convicted of anti-Soviet propaganda for the second time in 1975, for editing *Veche*, a Russian nationalist journal. Osipov was sentenced to eight years in a strict-regimen camp.

Petras Paulaitis, a Lithuanian Latin teacher and Ph.D., born in 1904, was a wartime resistance leader against the Germans. His loyalties to his own people brought on him heavy Soviet retribution. Credited with being active in saving Lithuanian Jews and escaping from a German concentration camp, Paulaitis was also active in resisting the Soviet occupation of Lithuania until a war tribunal sentenced him in 1946 to twenty-five years' imprisonment. He was released in 1956 after his case was reviewed, but had to work as a stoker in a Kaunas canning factory because authorities would not allow him to teach unless he renounced "bourgeois nationalism." In 1957 he was again arrested, convicted of subversive activities among the students of the Kaunas Polytechnic Institute, and returned to camp to serve the remainder of his sentence, to which another twenty-five-year term was added in 1958, making him eligible for release—at the age of seventy-nine—in 1983. A 1960 decree making fifteen years the maximum prison term in most cases was not applied to Paulaitis or a number of other political prisoners whose offenses (treason or anti-Soviet agitation) are considered especially grave.

Viktoras Petkus, a Lithuanian Catholic activist and church sexton, was a member of the Lithuanian Helsinki Watch Group. He had been arrested in 1947, probably for Catholic youth activities, and in 1957 was arrested for "anti-Soviet propaganda" and sentenced to seven years in prison. He was arrested again on August 24, 1977, convicted in July 1978, and sentenced to ten years' imprisonment and five years' internal exile.

Evgeny Pronyuk, a worker at the Institute of Philosophy of the

Ukrainian Academy of Sciences, was arrested in Kiev in July 1972, during a period of widespread repression against Ukrainian intellectuals. He was sentenced to seven years of camp and five years of exile on charges of "anti-Soviet propaganda" in November 1973, and is now in a Perm strict-regimen camp.

Father Vasily Romanyuk, an Orthodox priest from the village of Kosmach (in the Western Ukraine), was first arrested in 1944 at the age of nineteen on suspicion of having contacts with Ukrainian nationalists. "They [the local Ukrainian Communists] painted me as a nationalist-cleric and that was enough for them to give me ten years," he has written. "My parents were exiled to Siberia, where my father died from the unbearable labor and hunger, and my little brother was killed by a Communist punitive expedition just because he ran out of the house when they took the family away." Although he was sentenced a second time, still in camp, on a charge of anti-Soviet agitation and propaganda, he was later rehabilitated until his arrest in early 1972 and subsequent sentence to two years in prison, five years in special-regimen camp, and three years in exile, presumably for having protested Valentin Moroz' conviction, but possibly on account of his sermons.

Mykola Rudenko, a fifty-eight-year-old Ukrainian writer and wounded war veteran, was chairman of the Helsinki Watch Group in the Ukraine and a former member of the Ukrainian Writers Union and the Communist Party. He circulated his own *samizdat* critique of Marxism as well as Watch Group documents. Arrested in February 1977, he was sentenced that July for "anti-Soviet agitation and propaganda" to seven years' strict regime and five years' internal exile.

Maria Semyonova, born in 1925, is reportedly serving a third sentence for belonging to the True Orthodox Church, a religious sect branded illegal by the Soviet authorities. Her second ten-year term of imprisonment ended in October 1971, and she was believed to be back in a Mordovian camp in December 1974.

Felix Serebrov, a Russian former political prisoner, was a member of the Working Committee to Investigate Abuse of Psychiatry. He was sentenced in Moscow in October 1977 to one year in a forced-labor camp for having a forged labor book which did not show his previous conviction.

Aleksandr Sergienko, a Kiev artist and restorer, is one of a large number of Ukrainian intellectuals to suffer in the 1972 campaign to repress dissent in the Soviet Union's second-largest republic. Sentenced in June 1972 to seven years in prison camp and three in exile, he was found guilty of involvement in the "preparation" of "anti-Soviet" literature because he had made marginal notes in the *samizdat* manuscript of *Russification or Internationalism* by Ivan Dzyuba (London: Weidenfeld & Nicholson, 1968). (The book's author received a five-year sentence in March 1972.) Sergienko was further charged with having *spoken* of the Ukraine's right to self-determination and having protested the 1968 invasion of Czechoslovakia. Sergienko was transferred in December 1973—as a punishment—from the Perm camps to Vladimir Prison, where he was put in a punishment cell on occasion despite a history of chronic pulmonary tuberculosis. In January 1977, he was returned to Perm (strict regimen) Camp 36.

Rafkat Shaimukhamedov, of Przhevalska in the Kirghiz SSR, was executed for allegedly robbing a produce shop and murdering the sales clerk. He was convicted on the basis of testimony given by his alleged accomplices, Sultanov and Zharkov. Sultanov turned himself in to the police the day after the crime and identified Shaimukhamedov as its "organizer and perpetrator." Although Zharkov was the only one who supposedly spoke during the robbery, witnesses claimed to identify Shaimukhamedov by his voice. The material proof used to convict was blood found on Shaimukhamedov's trousers, but according to the court's medical experts, it was not the blood of the deceased. The shoes and clothing of his "accomplices" were not even submitted for analysis, and the court also did not question witnesses who had spoken with the dying victim or with neighbors who could have provided Shaimukhamedov with an alibi. Sultanov and Zharkov were sentenced to eight-year and five-year prison terms, respectively. Rafkat Shaimukhamedov maintained his innocence both during the investigation and at the trial, and later refused to petition for a pardon. On death row, he went on a four-month hunger strike, demanding—in vain—a new investigation. All his mother's attempts to get her son a new trial were rebuffed also. In all, she received twenty form-letter assertions from the USSR Procuracy denying that any grounds existed to justify reopening the case.

Anatoly Shcharansky, born in 1948, a computer scientist, Jewish "refusednik," and member of the Moscow Helsinki Watch Group, was arrested on March 15, 1977, and accused of espionage. The charge was apparently based on his connections with foreign correspondents, in particular Robert Toth of the Los Angeles *Times.* He was convicted in July 1978 and sentenced to thirteen years of imprisonment despite protests from governments, nongovernmental organizations, Nobel laureates, and other influential individuals in the West.

Yaroslav Shkraba, from the far-eastern port city of Khabarovsk, was eighteen when he died in October 1976 while an Army conscript. Like many Baptists, he had accepted enlistment but had refused to take the army's service oath. Only after appealing to the Procuracy and to Soviet leader Leonid Brezhnev did his parents receive their son's body, in a zinc coffin which they were ordered not to open. The parents disobeyed, however, and found that their son's body had been burned in places and that there were traces of blows to his head. Afterward, the commander of military section 64571 asked Shkraba's father to corroborate the official report of death by river drowning and to stop further investigation into the matter.

Danilo Shumuk, born December 30, 1914, in the Ukrainian village of Boremche in Volyn, was first arrested in 1931 as a Communist and jailed for eight years by Polish authorities, then sentenced at the end of the war by a Soviet tribunal to twenty years for his wartime partisan activities. While serving that term in the Norilsk camps, he became one of the organizers of a prisoners' uprising in June 1953, and was sentenced to death. That sentence commuted, he was freed in 1956 only to be rearrested back in the Ukraine and sentenced on May 5, 1958, to ten years in a strict-regimen camp in Mordovia for anti-Soviet agitation and propaganda. For writing and distributing his memoirs after his release, Shumuk was arrested again in January 1972, in Boguslavl (near Kiev), where he worked as a watchman in a children's camp, and sentenced on July 7 to ten years in a special-regimen camp and five years in exile.

Mikhail Shtern, an endocrinologist in Vinnitsa, was sentenced on the last day of 1974 to an eight-year prison-camp term for extorting bribes from his patients. The witnesses at his trial, however, gave to many observers the appearance of having been coerced into testifying against a respected physician whose real sin—in the eyes of the Soviet authorities—was the permission he had given his grown sons to emigrate to Israel. His trial, used as a warning to other would-be émigrés and their relatives, occasioned a great deal of public protest in the West. On the eve of what was to have been an "International Tribunal" giving publicity to his case, Soviet authorities announced in March 1977 that his sentence had been reduced (because of his good conduct, advanced age, and illness) to the time already served (two years, nine months). Dr. Shtern was freed and allowed to leave the USSR.

Sergei Soldatov, a forty-five-year-old Russian engineer, was active in the Estonian Democratic Movement. He was sentenced in 1975 for "anti-Soviet agitation and propaganda" to six years' strict regimen in a forced-labor camp.

Gabriel Superfin is a Moscow historian and literary scholar. Two months after the conviction of Viktor Khaustov (q.v.), the same Orel court sentenced Superfin, who had been arrested in July 1973, to five years in a strict-regimen camp—much of it actually spent in Vladimir Prison—and two years in exile. Among other things, Superfin was charged with collecting and preparing materials for *The Chronicle of Current Events;* editing that journal and a book based on it, *Uncensored Russia,* by Peter Reddaway (New York: American Heritage Press, 1972); and writing letters on behalf of the "Trial of the Four" defendants.

Ivan Svitlichny, a literary critic, was arrested in Kiev in January 1972, during a period of wide-scale repression against Ukrainian intellectuals. He was sentenced to seven years of camp and five years of exile on charges of "anti-Soviet agitation and propaganda" in April 1973, and is now in a Perm strict-regimen camp.

Mindaugas Tamonis was a thirty-five-year-old Lithuanian engineer whose body was found a few days after Stase Lukshaite's (q.v.) death near some Vilnius railroad tracks (a supposed suicide). He had been first forcibly confined to a psychiatric hospital and given insulin shock therapy for refusing in April 1974 to put up a monument in Lithuania to the "Red Army—Liberator" and declaring that he wanted self-determination and a multiparty system for the once-independent state. In June 1975, he was recommitted for about two months—during which time his mother died of a heart attack—after he sent a letter to the Lithuanian Communist Party's Central Committee warning of the threat of neo-Stalinism and urging the development of Christian culture in Lithuania.

Oleksei Tykhy, a fifty-one-year-old Ukrainian schoolteacher, was a member of the Ukrainian Helsinki Watch Group. He was sentenced in 1957 to seven years in forced-labor camp for circulating *samizdat* documents, and sentenced again in 1977, for "anti-Soviet propaganda" for circulating Watch Group documents, to ten years in a special-regimen camp and five years' internal exile.

Georgy Vins is the secretary of the Council of Evangelical Christian-Baptist Churches, an organization unrecognized and persecuted by Soviet authorities. He was first sentenced to three years in prison camp in 1966 for violating the laws on the separation of church and state and church and school and imprisoned again in January 1975 for five years in a strict-regimen camp for his role as secretary of the "illegal" religious grouping and for organizing the church publication *The Christian*, and the Council of Relatives of imprisoned ECB Church members, as well as for drafting the ECB Church Council charter and compiling Biblical textbooks.

Pyotr Vins, twenty-one-year-old son of imprisoned Baptist leader Georgy Vins, and a member of the Ukrainian Helsinki Watch Group, was tried and sentenced to one year in labor camp on a charge of "parasitism" on April 6, 1978.

Index